UPWARD

UPWARD

LEADERSHIP LESSONS FOR
WOMEN ON THE RISE

EDITED AND COMPILED BY

Bridgett McGowen-Hawkins
and Simone E. Morris

BMcTALKS Press
4980 South Alma School Road
Suite 2-493
Chandler, Arizona 85248

Published by BMcTALKS Press, a division of BMcTALKS, LLC, Chandler, Arizona.

BMcTALKS Press is an independent publishing company that provides a full suite of publishing services to new authors with an emphasis on professional speakers, professional coaches, entrepreneurs, and small business owners.

Volume pricing is available to bulk orders placed by corporations, associations, and others. For details, please contact BMcTALKS Press at info@bmtpress.com or 202.630.1218.

FIRST EDITION

Library of Congress Control Number: 2021902193

Paperback ISBN: 978-1-953315-06-9
eBook ISBN: 978-1-953315-07-6

Cover design by Bogdan Matei.
Interior design by Medlar Publishing Solutions Pvt Ltd., India.

Printed in the United States of America.

For Jaidah, Chloe, and Millie

ACKNOWLEDGMENT

The publisher and the editors greatly appreciate the generous sponsorship by the following contributors—sponsorship that positioned us to provide stories, challenges, and advice from an especially broad range of leaders:

Lisa DeFalco
Sarah Jean Sagredo-Hammond
Heidi Solomon-Orlick
Lucy Sorrentini
Hope Phillips Umansky, PhD

CONTENTS

CONTENTS

PART ONE

PART TWO

PART THREE

CONTENTS

PREFACE

Have you ever searched and searched for a book that answers a burning question, but you come up empty-handed?

That's what happened to Bridgett McGowen-Hawkins, and that's how *Upward* came to be.

In February 2020, just before the pandemic took a firm grip on the world, virtually halting air travel and significantly changing the rules of social engagement, Bridgett met with a conference organizer, David, at one of her favorite Arizona breakfast eateries to discuss the prospect of her delivering a keynote address at one of his upcoming conferences. He and his wife were in town for baseball enthusiasts' much-anticipated annual event; they were in town for Spring Training, and David decided to mix in a little business while on the trip.

As she always does when presented with the opportunity to speak at an event, Bridgett asked plenty of questions about the upcoming conference to ensure she would be a good fit as a speaker and, more importantly, to ensure she could answer a question or address a challenge for the conference-goers.

Over steaming cups of the most delicious coffee ever and omelets cooked to perfection, David outlined an impressive line-up of conference-goers: mostly women who are all accomplished in their respective industries. As she listened, Bridgett took notes and silently thought "These ladies sound like they really have their acts together! What in the world can I offer them in a speech?!"

But it was this one comment from David, this one challenge that caught her attention and lingered in the air for her: Many of the women felt like they were on islands, all alone, trying to navigate their lives and the challenges that come with being leaders.

Immediately after the meeting, Bridgett commenced to searching for books that spoke to that challenge, books that contained real life stories from real life women detailing their paths to leadership, the challenges they have had to overcome, and advice they would proffer other leaders. She didn't find one.

It was at this point when it became clear what her next project would be, and it was easy to identify who would join her on this journey. Bridgett's best friend, CEO, author, speaker, and award-winning diversity and inclusion leader Simone E. Morris, was the obvious co-editor. They discussed and outlined their plan, then reached out to their networks, letting them know about their idea to compile a book about women leaders *for* women leaders with a publication date of March 8, 2021, International Women's Day.

And the ladies were totally on board! *Upward* contributors offer corporate, nonprofit, and independent entrepreneur perspectives in their answers the following questions:

1. What was your path to leadership? How did you find yourself in the leadership role you now hold?

2. What has been your greatest challenge as a leader, and how have you addressed it or overcome it?

3. What is your best advice you would give a woman in leadership or one who is ascending into a leadership role?

The goal of *Upward* is help women everywhere know they are not alone, that success looks different for everyone, and that the path to leadership is one that can surely be created and created on each lady's own terms.

Do you have a question you want answered in the form of a book? Is there a question you want to answer yourself? Get in touch with BMcTALKS Press at info@bmtpress.com, and let us get to work. Let us print your passion!

FOREWORD

Women leaders and change makers are all around us. As a female leader, it is my choices, my voice, my actions people are watching. Whether that influence is positive or negative is up to me. I choose to use my power of leadership to be a force for good for those around me.

This book contains inspirational stories of women who are making a difference in everyday lives around the world. Even though they come from different places, cultures, and backgrounds, they have similar leadership characteristics that I guarantee will inspire you.

Character counts, so honor it! The importance of character and integrity can't be overlooked in our everyday lives and careers. Character is the foundation of how you present yourself to the world. A leader's admirable character will influence others to be better. To honor this, compromise is not an option. Live by your moral or ethical character, and it will fundamentally shape how you engage with the world around you—what you notice, what you value, what you choose to act on, and how you make decisions. Make a positive impact, and it will have a ripple effect on those around you.

Be the force! In today's world of social media, we are always on stage. Be aware that you're being watched and followed every day. That means demonstrating the attitudes and behaviors you want to see in others. Walk the talk, and talk the walk. As you beam with perspective, integrity, passion, and resilience, let the light of your leadership bring out your best so you can be proud of who you are and who you inspire others to be.

Own it! Everyone makes mistakes—we are human. Own those mistakes and move on. When you show accountability for your actions, you will influence those around you to take responsibility for theirs. Don't make excuses and blame others. It's a form of bad leadership that creates a toxic environment and can lead to mistrust. People do business with and want to be around others whom they know, like, and trust. People are watching. This is your chance to be the leader that demonstrates to others how to handle both success and failure.

Remind yourself every day that your leadership is contagious. Your actions, words, attitude, and how you carry yourself are reflected unto others. Think and rethink how you show up. Don't lose yourself. Be who you really are and don't make excuses. Lead from within. Every time you exhibit motivating leadership to those who surround you, it moves us forward in creating a better world and presents us as the next agents of change. The world is watching. Be your best you!

Learn from these stories and the leaders within these pages to reveal your own force from within!

Terri Kimble
CEO, Chandler Chamber of Commerce
Chandler, Arizona
July 15, 2020

WHAT I WISH I'D KNOWN...

Bridgett McGowen-Hawkins

As I write this, it is 8:00 p.m. exactly on an excitingly cool Saturday evening in the Phoenix suburb of Chandler, Arizona. Specifically, it is November 7, 2020; America has just elected the 46th President of the United States, and for the first time ever, the world will see not only a person of color but a *woman* of color holding the position of Vice President of the United States.

The point?

To girls and women everywhere: Anything is possible.

Anything.

If you have an idea, spread it.

If you have a goal, pursue it.

If you have a dream, live it.

Let no one tell you that you cannot or that you will not grow, achieve, or shine. Instead, show everyone that you must and that you shall.

Ensure you move in silence. It is not necessary that everyone knows what you are doing or what you plan to do. Simply move, and let your actions speak—and speak loudly!—for themselves.

Will you have fears? Yes, but dig deep for the courage to press on.

Will you make mistakes? Absolutely! Remember to always identify the hidden lesson.

Will you need help? You'd better believe it! Surround yourself with those who are experts and who believe in your vision. You cannot and should not do everything. The smartest people have even smarter people on their team and in their midst.

Will you have doubts? You will, but don't get stymied; keep a trusted friend in your midst who will validate your feelings and who will reassure you that you can do this. (Also have a second friend who will be brutally honest with you and a third who will show you love no matter how horribly you fall short or screwed up.)

Be bold. Be brave. Ask for help when you need it. Surround yourself by those who love and support you. Accept no less than the finest for yourself. Insist on uplifting others. Be the best version of yourself. It's in you, and you know it. You simply have to let everyone else know it.

When it feels like fighting for a seat at the table is not a possibility or the prospect of bringing your own folding chair is not a reality, design and build your own dinette set! See no obstacles.

When I entered corporate America in 2009, after spending more than a decade teaching at three different institutions of higher education, I had no interest in becoming a member of the C-suite or wanting to become head of that department or executive director of this division. I loved what I did—making presentations!—and I simply wanted to be seen as a superstar for that, recognized for that, and handsomely paid for that!

In due time, though, I realized that the value I saw (and still see) in my expertise and in my areas of talent and interest did not align with the value corporate America placed on those talents and interests. Think about it: have you heard of a Chief Presentation Skills Officer? As such, there was seemingly no chair for me, and if I showed up with a folding chair, I'd get laughed out of the room. The solution? Create my own table and seating where I am recognized and appreciated for my genius, and I am compensated for it on my terms.

To the reader, I encourage you to opt for more than just a seat at the table because you deserve more. Put yourself at the head of the table, or if need be, create your own table. Oh, if decades ago, I'd known that and so much more....

I came into this world to win, but it took me a long time to realize that was a possibility or that that was even my goal, given the foundation I had. (That's another story for another book on another day!) I needed many signs. Many, many signs! Finally, after decades, I chose myself, and I chose my own path.

Did Kamala Harris choose the path of vice presidency? Did she unequivocally affirm, as a little girl, that that would be her destiny? Or did she simply *know* she would grow up to be a powerhouse and then chose to move in that direction?

Now, it's time for you to choose.

The very personal stories in the following pages offer a glimpse into each leader's world. You will see leadership that is not perfect but that each leadership path is perfectly designed for its go-getter.

Choose your path, lean into it, and get going!

–B

LETTER TO THE READER

Simone E. Morris

Dear Reader,

It has been my absolute pleasure to collaborate with the fabulous women in *Upward*. Their leadership stories deliver on the results of passion and perseverance. I feel sure you will gain wisdom to help you on your leadership journey, no matter your goal.

I encourage you to take the time to find and leverage your voice to change the world. As someone very passionate about creating more inclusive leaders and transforming workplace cultures, I know this investment in your development and growth is a worthwhile one.

Here are a few suggestions for how to add inclusion to your leadership toolkit.

1. Make diversity, equity, and inclusion a personal and professional priority.

2. Invest in growing your cultural competency. Create a professional development plan that is intent on building your inclusive leadership skills. Training on empathy and emotional intelligence are worthwhile investments.

3. Consume materials that build your self-awareness, courage, and vulnerability. Psychologist, Author, and Speaker, Brené Brown, sets an excellent example in her materials (books, talks, etc.). She encourages us to embrace vulnerability as a leadership asset. Let us do as she says and dare greatly on our leadership journey.

4. Find ways to hold yourself accountable on the inclusion journey.

    a. Join groups on social media that have a focus on building inclusive leadership skills

    b. Enlist an inclusion accountability coach

    c. Secure mentors/sponsors on your inclusion journey

    d. Test out your inclusion skills (speak and write about your lessons)

5. Celebrate your wins along the way. For, dear reader, they will be fuel for your journey.

My path to leadership included many twists and turns. Each experience brought me closer to standing in my truth. As a girl who emigrated from Jamaica to the United States, I had no clue that leadership was my future path. It wasn't until my junior year of college that leadership showed its face and encouraged me to be brave. It was my first introduction to diversity, equity, and inclusion, but I had no idea. I was a leader in the Black Student Union at Quinnipiac. I had no idea that there was hidden leadership potential. I brushed off the experience to focus on landing my first corporate role. Now, decades later, I can see that God had a plan for me, but it took me a long time to catch on.

When I did catch on, I learned several things:

1. Your career is your responsibility. Having this knowledge means acting accordingly to become aware of your strengths and weaknesses.

2. Remaining silent can hurt you. Even if you are an introvert, you have to find a way to courageously stand in your truth. I suggest Toastmasters as an option for building confidence.

3. Find yourself sponsors who are willing to help you become the leader you want to be. Yes, I wrote *"sponsor."* Your success team should include mentors, sponsors, allies, champions, and more. Do not stop at mentor. I made that mistake, and my leadership transformational journey took the long and windy road.

4. Leverage success communities to immerse yourself in growing your leadership skills. Check out Facebook Groups that support your interests and passion. I have had luck with Ladies Who Leverage and Women Helping Women Entrepreneurs.

5. Embrace the discomfort of risk to gain greater success—volunteer for leadership roles that will stretch you and grow your capabilities as a leader.

6. Learn how to deal with rejection and people or situations that disappoint you.

7. Keep going and you will make your intentional mark on the world. There will be times when you're ready to throw in the towel, but give yourself grace when these moments arise. Experience the emotions and then revisit to make a decision that you can live with.

8. Create a generous annual budget for your leadership development. Tap into it to get the support you need to be successful.

9. Be kind to yourself on your leadership journey.

10. Remember how to play and have fun, or it will be a dull journey. Strive to have a balance of work, play, and family. You've got one life to live. Enjoy it.

I wish you success on the journey upward.

Warmly,
Simone

PART ONE

SILENCE THE CRITICS TO CREATE A PATH FORWARD

Lisa DeFalco
CEO and Founder of TPG

LISA'S PATH TO LEADERSHIP

My path to leadership is not for the faint of heart. It involved as much failure as success, sprinkled with reflection and gratitude. Most of my childhood was spent in Newark, New Jersey, an inner-city environment where work was expected, and dreams were not. The most ambitious accomplishment I could muster was entrance into college, and I was the first in my family to graduate with a college degree.

I was an average and unsettled student in college, full of what I thought was ambition but too disorganized to capitalize on it. When I graduated, a friend offered me a job in a call center, and I simply took it to avoid having to create a résumé and start interviewing. I didn't want to think about my career. I simply accepted a form of income that would allow me to move into my own apartment and start the next chapter of my life. It wasn't long into that position that I began to feel unsettled again. I grew restless with the role I had in the company and sought advancement. Since it was a privately held company, advancement came quickly in the form of broadening my responsibilities to include areas of the business that needed attention or simply were not glamorous enough to hire a seasoned professional to lead.

I started as a supervisor. Within two years, I had become responsible for operations involving all labor shifts, overseeing about a dozen supervisors as well as HR and quality assurance. Yet, I still wanted more. Looking back on those years, I realize that my ambition was really nothing more than a yearning for something more in life—that continuous feeling of being unsettled. I had not really become ambitious yet, although from the outside it would appear that I was. I was simply a kid from the inner city trying to find my way and not feeling that I fit in anywhere I went. It was during these initial years in the working world that I transitioned from feeling unsettled to developing an ambition to serve a more purposeful mission in life. And I recall the day it all started....

Having been given more responsibility than my years deserved, I was also expected to do the work that no one else in senior leadership wanted to do. Much of that had to do with working long hours and engaging our front-line labor force. I learned quickly that my work ethic was my strongest characteristic—which probably remains true today. My energy made fifteen-hour workdays, without even a moment of hesitation, the norm. I thrived on the energy and pace. So when the company's owners announced my first defining assignment of leadership, I wanted to embrace it wholeheartedly. I wanted to embrace it with the same energy I gave every challenge. Yet, something was so direly wrong with the assignment that I privately struggled.

What was the assignment? Laying off the *entire* operation from Christmas Eve until the third week of January. We were a call center, but none of our customers wanted to pay us to make calls during that time. So, instead of carrying labor costs and impacting their own profits, the owners decided that everyone would be laid off. No salary, no paid time off, no nothing. I was asked to make the announcement on December 23 and process the paperwork for the entire staff—all 150 people. The owners advised me of this assignment a few days prior as they casually left the office to have dinner. I spent the next few days numb and feeling ill. I convinced myself that this decision was necessary for the company's survival. I figured that the owners would never lay off an entire workforce on Christmas Eve unless it was absolutely necessary, and this temporary closing would ensure we could financially return in January. So, as a completely inexperienced twenty-three-year-old, I held my first all-company meeting to share the news. People cried. I was ice about it. I knew it had to be done and simply completed the task. Was that the lesson in leadership? No, it was not. It was a lesson in cowardice. But I didn't know it at the time.

We did return in January and the operation grew. We started a third production shift, thereby expanding our hours of operation from 9:00 a.m. to midnight. We operated seven days a week. There was never a day that went by without work, and I thrived on the pace. As the following year came to a close, I thought for certain we would celebrate the growth, the "above and beyond" effort the entire team had put forth to grow to 260 employees in our operation. We operated every waking hour available to call centers in those days, and the owners were generating a 50% margin for every hour we worked. Definitely worthy of recognition, right? Once again, as Christmas Eve approached, I was advised that the company would shut down until the third week of January. Once again, I was told to lay off the entire company on Christmas. This time I pushed for pay for the team, paid time off, a year-end bonus, or even a simple symbolic thank-you gift. All requests were denied.

That is when my lesson took hold. This time, as I gathered my team to share this news, I cried with them. I listened to the stories of our working moms who were unsure how they were going to provide Christmas for their kids. I heard the pain in their voices as they talked about the impact of being without income for a month. I learned that leadership is about showing up and facing the difficult moments. I learned not to delegate the meaningful moments that could build up a culture or tear it down. Leadership creates a culture, and it is during the darkest times that an inspiring culture can be formed. That's leadership; that's the lesson that I took as I left to start my own company.

Starting your own enterprise in your twenties is no easy feat. While I started my own business with this memorable lesson, I still lacked any senior business experience associated with creating a company. Over the past twenty-four years, I have "learned on the field," as they say. Every experience teaches me a lesson. I consider myself a student of life and business. The guiding light that has always led me involves the power of leading a team by a vision that creates a purpose greater than any one individual. This powerful lesson started on a Christmas week, when I realized that we were all in the situation together, that we all sought a way to do well for the company we worked for while doing well for our families. This spirit of togetherness helped me through the second season of personnel cuts and confirmed my desire to create a place where that belief—the belief that we were all in the situation together—truly mattered. That was the fuel behind opening the doors to my own organization. That purpose remains the fuel behind my passion, even now.

Creating a common purpose to unify a group of people requires constant communication of what your vision is, as well as humility to know when you are not living up to those expectations. That's a hard lesson to learn in your twenties. I found myself learning that lesson for *decades*. As I said, I'm a student in this game of life and business.

When people ask about the single greatest experience that helped me become the leader that I am, I share the following without hesitation: failure. I have failed more than I have succeeded. I used to fear failure. Over time, I learned that it is part of the path of success. I cannot recognize or celebrate the great success we have experienced at TPG without having lived through the failures. There are highs and lows in business. That rhythm allows for reflection during the lows and gratitude during the highs. When you start to embrace that rhythm and allow it to truly become part of your DNA, then you learn the power of reflection and gratitude, regardless of the moment that you are experiencing. As a result, I also find gratitude during the darkest moments and reflect during our greatest accomplishments.

These past few years at TPG have involved several new twists in uncharted territory, including managing through a global pandemic.

Yes, there are highs and lows, but now each ride up the proverbial roller coaster ushers in peace versus exuberance, and each downward twist brings humility instead of despair. While my title of CEO and Founder suggests a leadership role, it is my ability to lead with reflection and gratitude that allows me to humbly accept the title of leader.

LISA'S GREATEST CHALLENGE

Not knowing my own voice or direction…not having enough quiet in my life to silence the noise involving fear and belief that I cannot do something.

The greatest challenge faced by any leader, especially women, is not having a strong inner voice to guide one along the path forward. As women, we are taught to mind our manners and listen before speaking. Consciously or subconsciously, we are taught to heed the words of others, as the men in our lives are taught to lead. I was raised by a very strong woman, and even she succumbed to the noise around her at many points in her life. As such, we are placed in roles to define our behavior even though they should be seen simply as options to the many paths available to us in life. As a woman in business, I find these roles create a different message than the one I silently yearn to develop for myself. The message is that societal conflict creates an automatic group of critical voices that compete with my inner voice of who I am and the path I choose to pursue.

The "battle" between external influences and my inner voice rages on even today. There are too many critics in the world, and they show up at the most inopportune times—moments when your uncertainty is high. They are happy to share why an idea won't work or pick at your greatest insecurity, like a child picks at a scab.

Some of these critics do particular harm because they position their feedback with words of false support, in the spirit of "helping." Without having a strong inner voice and belief system, it is easy to lose your direction and wind up overwhelmed.

I've experienced great success at TPG but also significant hardships. My inner voice is needed during both cycles to guide me as an individual and a leader. The two are one and the same. I have learned that when my individual soul is lost, then everything around me feels unknown. When I can't recognize myself, I can't recognize my surroundings, which opens me up to poor choices and the opinion of those whose counsel is not authentic.

Several years ago, TPG lost a significant client, which caused us to reduce our workforce by 40%. It was a brutal experience and one of the greatest professional failures in my life. We had just agreed to move into a new corporate headquarters, signing a fifteen-year lease for millions of dollars. The client loss triggered financial losses that needed to be addressed rapidly to avoid collapse. At the same time, historical memories of how *not* to handle a business downturn stewed in my mind. We worked with our HR team to offer everyone severance and several months of notification that the change would occur. The decision to provide severance, manage through this downturn, and work to secure new clients became the clear path. But that path was not without its critics. Nor would it be the last time that the voice of critics rang so loudly in my ears that I had to silence them in order to lead us forward.

The most recent experience of COVID-19 probably gives the best example of the need to have a strong inner voice. Like most companies, we experienced revenue reduction. Clients asked for assistance to modify their spend commitments with us, yet we had just decided to embark on an extensive research and development (R&D) investment in AI technology for our business. It appeared that the timing was all wrong for that investment and we should hold off until the following year. Concurrently, our staff was becoming growingly concerned about working from the office. The amount of duress was palpable. One day I looked at the calendar and it was March 15; the next time I looked up it was July—a blur.

There were a number of decisions I was required to make during that time. Moving our workforce home, gracefully agreeing to client revenue reductions, managing the nerves of our staff, renegotiating our office rent, deciding on the continuation of our R&D investment, deciding whether or not to lay off staff since we now found ourselves more than twenty-five people overstaffed, and deciding when to return to our office were just a few of the tough calls that required my attention. Deliberating on these issues required all of the past experience I have learned about reflection, gratitude, tenacity, and perseverance. This was the most monumental moment of TPG's tenure and my career. How I navigated this would impact us for years. What did I need most? Quiet. I needed to hear what my inner voice was sharing. I had the advice of the outside from a variety of perspectives, but the voice I counted on the most was my own, so I had to find it.

I sought my inner voice among a sea of noise. Feedback and fear were everywhere, especially as the pandemic accelerated. I had my share of critics in the galley. I'd been called reckless, uncaring, indecisive, and inexperienced, as well as compassionate, thoughtful, mature, strong, bold, and brave. I don't know which label best described me during this time, but I do know that I did not realize how little quiet I had in my life prior to COVID-19 and how much clearer the proper direction presented itself in that quiet. It was this new-found quiet that played the hero role during this chaos. In that quiet, I found my inner voice, and it was clear: push forward with our plans; make a bold play toward the future; don't succumb to fear that is surrounding everyone.

So we did. We retained employees, we set up home offices, we partnered with our primary landlord to release the pressure from our rent commitment, and most importantly, we doubled down on our R&D investment strategy to create the next generation of our company. When the pandemic panic clears, we stand ready to serve our clients with a business that will guide them into the next decade. We were decisive because, in the quiet, the direction forward appeared.

LISA'S BEST ADVICE

Be authentic…Be grateful…Be beautifully you.

Of all of the advice that I share with women in leadership—actually to all those who aspire to be their best selves—I believe gratitude and authenticity are the wisest. The beauty of entering one's 40s and 50s is that we start to become super-comfortable in our own skin. We start to see our beauty, even as fine lines appear on our face. We see our strength and how much we shine because of it. We see our weaknesses and embrace them as our vulnerable attributes worthy of love. We basically learn to see ourselves. I wish that for all of us. The faster that women in business start the journey of gratitude and authenticity, the faster they rise. Because, in the end, people are attracted to people. If you are a ray of light, people will be drawn to you in business and life. I found my ray by simply being Lisa. The more I learn about her, the more I like. The more the world sees her, the more embraced she becomes. The more I focus on how grateful I am to know the authentic Lisa, and the welcoming she receives, the more successful I feel.

That is probably the advice we all need to hear as we ascend into leadership roles. If we use reflection and gratitude as the common principles that unite us and we recognize that any effort worth taking requires tenacity and perseverance, then we are left to be our authentic selves. We can apply a style that is uniquely our own, without any sense of obligation to fit into a particular description established externally.

ABOUT LISA

Lisa DeFalco is the founder of TPG, Inc. and the Independent Quality Assurance market, making her an industry pioneer in what is known in the market by the tagline "this call may be monitored for quality assurance." In establishing the Quality Assurance market, TPG has become the recognized leader in consumer experience assessment throughout the largest global corporations across nine countries and eleven languages.

Lisa has more than twenty-nine years of experience assessing contact-center interactions, diagnosing quality gaps, and improving communications to drive business returns for her Fortune 500 clients. Lisa has worked to establish a diagnostic product methodology that would result in the creation of a linguistic model that is statistically linked to corporate performance indicators (to allow for predictive business intelligence modeling), the first of its kind and what really makes TPG standout in the marketplace. Lisa's expertise is the result of years of call-listening experience coupled with hands-on contact center improvement experience. Having conducted supervisor and agent training, calibration, and coaching in more than seventy contact centers for more than forty business-process-outsourcing (BPO) and other corporations throughout her career, she has gained significant insight on how to affect behavioral change with the insight gleaned from customer-experience linguistic diagnostics.

Prior to her launch in the Quality Assurance market, Lisa was a tenacious, committed, and ambitious girl from Newark, New Jersey. She has built an empire from scratch and believes that with hard work, grit, and grace, success like this could be for anyone who chooses.

Today, Lisa serves as TPG's Chief Executive Officer and its Chief Product Designer, guiding TPG's product teams in the integration of AI into their platforms as well as their design and delivery of products that valuate, analyze, activate, and optimize customer experience.

FAIL FAST AND TAKE MORE RISKS

Heidi Solomon-Orlick
Founder and CEO, GirlzWhoSell
Founder and CEO, Women's Impact Network
Vice President of Global Sales, VXI Global Solutions

HEIDI'S PATH TO LEADERSHIP

The year was 1977. Like so many other high school seniors, I had goals and dreams but did not have a firm grasp on where life was going to take me. During that year, I was competing for a coveted spot on the U.S. Equestrian Team. I had been training and riding competitively since early childhood. I knew that the competition was going to be tough, but that didn't deter me. I knew that I had only the one hour that was handicapped with hip dysplasia. I knew that I was competing nationally against others who had many more resources than I. None of that mattered. I was confident that I had both the talent and skill set to overcome those challenges. I had the grit, determination, and focus to push through any difficulty or obstacle that might come my way.

Bertalan de Némethy was the coach of the United States Equestrian Team show-jumping squad. He was a legend—bigger than life and someone I admired tremendously from afar. He was also that year's judge of the Olympic Trials that took place in California at Foxfield Riding School where I trained. The trials were three days of grueling horse-riding gymnastics, which ended with Mr. de Némethy calling me to the side of the ring to speak with him privately. I didn't know what to expect, but as I walked over to meet with him, my confidence and resolve immediately dissolved into panic and butterflies. He stoically introduced himself and told me that he thought I had a lot of "raw" talent. He then asked how many horses I had available to me if I were to make the team. I stared at him blankly, not quite understanding the enormity of the moment. I told him that I had only the one horse, which I did not actually own, but should I make the team, I am sure that I could find more horses somehow, some way. I honestly had no idea how I would actually make that reality happen, but I knew that I had to convince him; or I would lose this once in a lifetime opportunity. I had to sell him on me and my ability to obtain what was needed to be a successful and contributing member of the team. He smiled, shook his head, thanked me, and walked away. My heart sank.

While I was selected as an alternate, I did not make the Olympic team that year. Instead, I graduated from high school and decided to go to college. In retrospect, it may have been a blessing, as the United States boycotted the 1980 Olympics, and I would not have been able to compete, regardless. But, at the time, I was devastated and felt like a failure. As I reflect back on that moment, I realize the importance of being able to think quickly and adapt to situations on the fly. I recognize the true value of preparation and the need for the ability to overcome objections. I learned the significance of being able to tell a story and to being able to create and sell the value of a proposition and solution, regardless of the obstacles. It became clear to me that the stronger the solution, the better the outcome. All of these are critical components of sales success. This was my first real life foray into sales and a leadership lesson I would carry with me throughout my career.

Despite my inner confidence, I understood all too well that success was not a guarantee. In order to achieve success, I had to work hard at it. I did not grow up in the generation where everyone was a winner, and every person received a ribbon just for partic-ipation. Competing was black and white: you won, or you didn't. One thing that being in competitive sports taught me was that winning and/or losing was not always objective and not always fair. There were way too many things outside of my control that could impact the final result. For that reason, I opted to focus on the areas of my life that I could positively influence and impact. I did not unilaterally define my self-worth by whether I won or lost or by what others said or thought of me. I realized early on that their perceptions were more of a reflection on them than they were on me. Trying to change their perceptions was not deserv-ing of my time or my energy. Instead, I was—and still am—the judge and jury of my own life. Only I get to decide if I win or lose, and it is not based on whether I bring home the ribbon or the trophy, close the deal, or pass the finish line but is solely based on whether I did my absolute best, regardless of the outcome. That is how I define true success.

While in college, I decided to take a year off to get practical experience in advertising. I knew that the ad agency business was a highly male-dominated profession. I felt the need to do a test drive to see if advertising was the career path I should follow post-graduation. In the early 1980s, there were very few female role models in advertising, let alone executive leadership, except for Mary Wells Lawrence. Ms. Wells was the founding president of Wells, Rich, Greene, an advertising agency known for its award-winning creative work. She was the first female co-founder and CEO of a company, which later was listed on the New York Stock Exchange. I knew in my gut that I had to work for her, and so I picked up the phone and called her. As I think back on that pivotal moment, I know how insane that must have seemed back then because I know how crazy it even sounds today.

After some convincing, I was able to get through the gatekeeper and schedule a face-to-face meeting with her. When I entered her office, I was starstruck. She was glamorous, fierce, and brilliant. She had a way of motivating people to greatness. Men respected and admired her, and women wanted to be her. Following that meeting, I was hired to work as an assistant in the company's media-buying department despite my being young and not yet having my degree. She saw something in me that I didn't even see in myself.

I was assigned to the Jack-in-the Box account and had the privilege of being a part of the team that created the historic "blow up the clown" campaign amongst others. In the eighteen months I worked for the company, Ms. Wells asked me to sit in strategy meetings, be a part of task forces and thought leadership teams, and encouraged me to take on responsibility outside of the role for which I was hired. She taught me that in order to get promoted, you already had to be doing the work. She educated me on the importance of being a role model and of having someone to mentor, sponsor, and guide you. She coached me on the significance of succession planning, and that meant, as a future leader, it would be my responsibility to recognize and develop emerging talent. It would be incumbent upon me to one day pay it forward. But most of all, she inspired a leadership style that, to this day, I follow and admire. She did not give up her femininity to be a leader; she used the innate strengths of her femininity to succeed, including consensus building, open and honest communication, and vulnerability paired with strength. She encouraged me to return to college and complete my degree. I am indebted to her for the impact she had on my career, and it is likely she will never know it. Because of her influence, I promised myself that I would support, nurture, and mentor other women once I was in a position to do so. I decided that I would be a successful businesswoman in a man's world, despite the odds, not by imitating men, but by leading like a woman. Failure was not an option.

After graduating with Bachelor of Arts in Journalism and Speech Communications, I officially entered the field of advertising. Despite my prior experience, I started at the bottom as a receptionist (which was humbling) but was fast tracked into account management, sales, direct marketing, and executive leadership, all before the age of thirty. I had three-martini lunches with top industry executives (yes, that was a thing). I worked on cruise-line accounts, sailing the world on marketing trips, and launched the first master-planned community in Irvine, California, which changed the course of real estate. I sold to international clients, attended industry parties, and hobnobbed with Los Angeles's rich and famous. And I burned out. Over a ten-year period, I blew through three engagements, made several job changes, and lost my way.

It is interesting the decisions one makes after having, in some ways, hit the proverbial bottom. While on the outside I epitomized the definition of success, I was unhappy, dissatisfied, and unfulfilled. While I had started my own agency with a partner and continued to climb the career ladder, my life was spiraling downward out of my control. I had lost myself, and I had forgotten what was really important. I was searching for the key to self-fulfillment and joy, but I had no balance and had isolated myself from friends and close family. I had forgotten who I was and had compromised the values I held sacred. It was time to regroup and make a change. I decided to take a personal and professional risk and exit advertising. Without one look back, I put that life behind me. I did not know what my next career move would be. What I did know was that if I did not pivot and head down a different path, things would end badly. Sometimes just knowing you need to make a change is the thing that brings change into your life.

It was a warm Sunday afternoon. I had been out of work for three months and was living on my savings in a small apartment in Brentwood, California. I was happier than I had been in years. I walked into the Rose Tattoo Café for brunch, and there he was—a friend I had not seen since college. Over omelets, we brought each other up to speed on our lives. He had dropped out of college and founded a start-up telemarketing company, which was generating, at that time, $14 million in annualized revenue. I told him that after ten years in advertising and at thirty years old, I was unemployed, unmarried, and actively looking for a new career. Right there, on the spot, he offered me a job to come work for him as his Vice President of Sales. I told him that while I sincerely appreciated the offer, I could not accept the position because I did not have any prior outsourcing experience, and I did not know anything about the telemarketing industry. I realize now what a "girl thing" that is.

As women, we feel a need to have all our *i*s dotted and *t*s crossed before we can start or even apply for a job. And since that work—just like success—is always under construction, we never take the first step, we never leave the gate, we stop ourselves from taking risks. Thankfully, he was not going to let that happen.

His response was classic. He said, "Heidi, don't say 'no' without thinking about it. And, please, don't worry about not having the experience. You have an amazing background. Frankly, none of us knows anything about the telemarketing business. We are figuring it out every day." The next day, I called him, and I accepted the job, which was the start of a thirty-year career. He went on to grow that start-up to well over a billion dollars in revenue. I often think about what would have happened to my life if I hadn't taken the risk simply because I thought I was not fully qualified for the position. What if he hadn't started the business, despite not having a full understanding of the industry? Both of our lives would have been significantly different.

Since that day, my life has taken many twists and turns. After four years with that company, I left California, got married to my soulmate and best friend, raised three amazing children, and became a female trailblazer in business-process outsourcing (BPO) and technology sales. It has not always been easy, and I was often the only woman at the table; but even when times were tough, I never compromised my values or my femininity. In fact, that was my superpower! I often joke that when asked what I was going to be when I grew up, I never imagined that I would end up as a female sales executive in an industry dominated by men. I never envisioned that I would be balancing a life of corporate and entrepreneurship, waking up every day, thinking about how to make the world a more equitable place for future generations of young women. I never anticipated that I would be breaking through glass ceilings before women ever recognized there WAS a ceiling to shatter. What I realize now is that this is what I was destined to do. I realize how the pivotal moments I shared (and the many others I will leave for a different time and place) have had a defining impact on my life. All of these collective moments and experiences have culminated in my ability and desire to lead, inspire, and mentor other women. I am motivated and empowered to utilize the practical sales skills that I learned as a competitive athlete. I am inspired to emulate the other female (and male) role models I was blessed to have while growing up and to have known throughout my career. I am motivated by the desire to pave the way for the brave, brilliant, and immensely talented women who are working their way up the ranks behind me. It is our job as female leaders to create room for others, to remove obstacles, and to make the world a better place—a place where all people who identify as female have the opportunity to succeed, regardless of race, sexual orientation, or economic background. That is my mission, and I will not rest until I am satisfied that I have done everything in my power to affect change.

HEIDI'S GREATEST CHALLENGE

Throughout my forty-year professional career, I have faced many challenges that have tested my resolve. That stated, I think it is safe to assert that 2020 was among the most difficult years of my lifetime. The impact of the pandemic has been felt by people and companies around the world and has had an exponential and negative impact on women in particular. The resilience, ingenuity, and response, while often controversial, have been extraordinary. As state so beautifully by United CEO, Oscar Munoz, "As much as the pandemic has mandated from our society, it has revealed just as much about people. Far from causing division and discourse, our social distancing, quarantine, and forced remote work have allowed us to witness something profound: the innate need to be connected with one another."

According to American psychologist and spiritual leader, Tara Brach, "The spiritual path is not a solo endeavor. In fact, the very notion of a self who is trying to free her or himself is a delusion. We are in it together and the company of spiritual friends helps us to realize our interconnectedness."

As leaders, this new form of "interconnectedness" has forced us to evaluate our leadership styles and strategies. The global crisis has guided and inspired us to lead and connect in new and different ways. During and following the 2020 crisis, we have to look at and systematically dissect the current models of leadership and work together to create a transformed leadership playbook. For me, this is the most inspiring leadership challenge to date.

I want you to pause and think about the best leaders with whom you have ever worked. What did he or she do or say that inspired you, that motivated you, that led you to be the best version of yourself? I am sure each reader will have different examples of what worked and what didn't, but I would venture to conclude that some common themes are as follows: they cared, they listened, they were authentic, and they were empathic. Ironically, these are the natural skills of women.

In a recent study conducted by Forbes on the personality traits of the top 100 Most Powerful Women (Leaders) in the World, and according to the IBM Watson™ Personality Insights model, there are five core characteristics (appropriately named the "Big Five") that help define how a person engages with the world. These include *agreeableness, conscientiousness, extraversion, emotional range,* and *openness.* Each of these personality facets helps individualize a person's values, actions, and style of leadership.

Across the Forbes list, *openness* was the most common personality trait of successful female executives and is described as "the extent to which a person is open to experiencing different activities; openness includes a person's imagination, artistic interests, and overall intellectual curiosity." And yet, despite possessing these embedded personality archetypes, women are still under-represented in many areas of business including, but not limited to, executive leadership.

As an example, it is a proven fact that women have the innate traits to be successful at B2B sales and leadership and that women actually out-produce their male counterparts in enterprise sales.

Despite the data, women still represent a disproportionately small percentage of these roles—only 36% in sales and 19% in sales leadership to be exact. Overlay different industry sectors and women of color, and the numbers are even more dismal. So, what is it that is holding us back?

I grew up in an era when girls were meant to be seen and not heard. We were sugar and spice and everything nice—except when we weren't, which was most of the time for me. I believe that the foundation for leadership starts in the family, not in the classroom. It was my parents, in particular my mother, who taught me leadership skills. She told me that being a leader is a lot like being a parent. When you give birth to or adopt a child (I was adopted), you have these optimistic views of how you are going to raise that child, how amazing you are going to be at it, and how you are going to avoid the mistakes of the generations that pre-ceded you. And yet, when you finally take on the role, you may find that it wasn't exactly what you thought, that it does not align with your expectations, and that it is much harder than you imagined. Don't get me wrong; my mother enjoyed being a parent (most of the time). It was just that being a parent in and of itself was not enough. Sometimes you kill yourself to climb the ladder and don't take time to enjoy the journey. And, when you finally achieve management status, the elation you thought you would feel once you got there is illusive. A feeling of self-worth and satisfaction does not come from obtaining the job or the title; it comes from knowing that you have a voice, a seat at the table, and a position of influence. It comes from knowing that you can affect change. How you use that influence directly correlates to your sense of accomplishment and satisfaction, and will ultimately drive your leadership effectiveness.

I learned many lessons from my parents who were an incredible influence and inspiration in my life. In November of 2019, within twelve days of each other, my mother and father passed away after sixty-four years of marriage. This unbearable loss forced me to take a look at the purpose of my life. How do I want to define myself? What impact do I want to make, what legacy do I want to leave, and how do I want to be remembered? Their deaths made me reevaluate my relationships with people and my priorities, and strangely enough, in the midst of a global crisis, their deaths made me rethink my own leadership style. You see, while my mother was a traditional stay-at-home mom, she taught me the impor-tance of independence. She taught me that honesty and integrity are the foundation for trust, and trust is to be earned. She taught me that a woman should always have her own money and that to be a great leader, like parenting, you need to have fierce loyalty and the innate desire to protect and guide others. She also taught me that openness—allowing yourself to be vulnerable—is not a weakness but a strength. These are the traits we must honor as leaders as we navigate the next normal. By leveraging these characteristics, we can unilaterally overcome any leadership challenge that presents itself.

HEIDI'S BEST ADVICE

I have lived my life with very few regrets. While I have had many successes, I have also made my share of mistakes and had many failures along the way! Interestingly, I might make some tweaks, but I don't think I would change much of anything, even if I had the option to do so. It is because of these experiences that I am the person I am today. I am grateful and blessed for the opportunities I have had and want to impart the shared wisdom and knowledge I have gained over the years to those following in my footsteps. It is through that lens that I provide this guidance for others ascending into a role of sales and leadership. The following are the five things I wish I had known before embarking on my own leadership journey:

1: *You are enough*

Determining our self-worth based on how we measure or stack up against others takes us down an endless rabbit hole of self-doubt. You know what I say to that? We need to silence our inner critic—that voice inside our head that says, "I can't, I'm not good enough" or "I don't have the skills." The inner voice that compares us with other people or says, "You don't have the right degree or the right training or the proper credentials." That inner voice that gives you the feeling of imposter syndrome: "What if they find out who I really am?"

Growing up, I had developed this perception that to be successful personally and professionally, I had to be perfect. Perfection was a prerequisite to obtain approval and to succeed. Over time, I realized that trying to achieve perfection—whatever that meant—was an unattainable task. And so, in my late twenties, I wrote a goodbye letter to perfect Heidi. I put perfect Heidi into a box where she belonged, and that was incredibly freeing. I realized that I did not have to be perfect to lead a team, to run a company, to be a successful executive, or to be a good wife and mother. As professional U.S. soccer player and motivational speaker, Amy Wambach, said, "Imperfect men have been empowered and permitted to run the world since the beginning of time. It is time for imperfect women to grant themselves permission to join them." You do not have to be perfect—just enough.

2: Fail fast

I have always said that the word FAIL means the First Attempt in Learning. If you are afraid of failure, you will never move forward, and you will not succeed. Failure is based on fear, and fear is paralyzing. Tony Robbins says that we are "wired for fear and worry. There is a highway to upset and a dirt road to happiness." Fear is a powerful and convincing emotion. But fear is not real; your presence of awareness is real. Repeat after me: in hope, we are fearless. So, how do we move through fear? We take action—any action. We put one foot in front of the other and take one step, one day at a time. It is through failure that we know we are growing and learning, and that knowledge makes us better leaders. You will fail; just fail fast, and move on!

3: Take more risks

By nature, I am risk averse. I think that is true of women in general. Avoiding risk is one of my biggest regrets because I missed out on several opportunities that could have been very beneficial for me and my family. They also could have been disastrous, but because I did not take the risk, I will never know. There was always a good reason not to take the jump: I am short on cash, I am pregnant, we are saving for [insert word here], I have a secure job, and so on and so forth. I see now that there are many benefits to taking risk and that risk taking does not need to happen in a vacuum. First and foremost, taking risk reduces the hold that the fear of failure can have over us. Other documented benefits from risk-taking are that it builds confidence, allows us to develop new skills, provides the opportunity to actively pursue success, spurs creativity, and offers the opportunity to change the course of our lives. In leadership, risk-taking is essential to learning and building new skills. So, toss the parachute, and take that jump.

4: Delegate

A common misconception and roadblock to good leadership or to starting a business is the perception that you have to do it all yourself. It is difficult to delegate, and we, as women, have a need to control our situation. To learn to lead, we need to learn how to follow and how to give up that control. It has been said that to be a great leader, we need to practice discipline, fearlessly take on more responsibility, develop situational awareness, inspire others, keep learning, resolve conflict, be a discerning listener, and (number one for me) check our bias at the door. The whole is greater than the individual parts. Together—not alone—we can innovate and change the trajectory of the world.

5: *Take care of yourself*

Having a focus on self-care is critical to the success of any leader and business owner. Admittedly, this is the pot calling the kettle black because wellness is an area that I need to work on personally. Over the years, and especially in the challenging times occurring as I write this, I have learned that taking the time to recharge is an important ingredient in the recipe for great leadership and individual growth. I encourage you to remember this as you move up the leadership path. Journal, meditate, take a bath or a walk, but be sure to replenish your soul.

Please, don't lose sight of yourself.

In conclusion, my parting words of wisdom are that you should take smart and calculated risks; don't be afraid to fail; stop comparing yourself to others; give up perfection; and by all means, take care of yourself so that you can take care of those around you. But mostly, be kind, pay it forward, mentor, and inspire others. That is the gift you have to give the world and the legacy you can leave. We are in charge of our destiny, and as leaders, it is incumbent upon us to grow and influence the next generation. In doing so, we will leave the world a little bit better than the way we found it.

ABOUT HEIDI

Heidi Solomon-Orlick is an accomplished business-process-outsourcing (BPO) industry executive and sales leader with over thirty years' experience in global B2B sales. She is the Founder of the Women's Impact Network (WIN), an organization addressing the unique needs of women over fifty and tackling ageism in the workplace. Through WIN, she is launching the first

annual Wisdom Warrior Summit in 2021. Heidi is a venture investor in women-, LGBTQI-, and minority-owned businesses and is a SheEO Activator. In 2016-17 Heidi served on the National Organizing Committee of the Women's March on Washington and was the Founder and Co-Chair of Women's March Pennsylvania. Heidi is passionate about mentoring and sponsoring future sales leaders. To that end, she is the Founder and CEO of GirlzWhoSell, an organization with a mission to close the gender gap in B2B sales and to develop the largest pipeline of diverse female sales talent. Heidi is a diversity, inclusion, and equity champion and a frequent keynote speaker on the topic. She is Chief Storyteller of Making of HERstory, a podcast focused on women's stories and the pivotal moments that shaped their lives. Heidi has three sons and currently lives in New Hampshire with her husband of twenty-six years.

GRIT: THE SECRET ROARING UNDERDOG OF TRUE LEADERSHIP

Hope Phillips Umansky, PhD
Educator; Principal and Owner, Innovations: Education Advocacy
Group, Inc, a niche educational and therapeutic strategic consultant
and advocate; or just a plain old English teacher

The life you save may be your own.
— Flannery O'Connor

"Go back?" he thought. "No good at all! Go sideways?
Impossible! Go forward? Only thing to do! On we go!"
So up he got, and trotted along with his little sword held
in front of him and one hand feeling the wall, and his
heart all of a patter and a pitter.
— (J. R. R. Tolkien, *The Hobbit: There*
and Back Again; a book of myths)

DR. HOPE'S PATH TO LEADERSHIP

Like everything in life, the path to leadership is nonlinear. It is at once full of every sad, tragic, and true story and every happy and cherished one. The path to leadership is one of being fully human. It is the story of "What happened?" Everything good and bad that could happen happened, and nothing in particular happened at all. Everything and nothing; nothing and everything.

When I was a little girl, people would ask, "What do you want to be when you grow up?" My answer was never, "I wanna be a leader!" It certainly was not the unimaginable word soup that is my career: "I want to be a higher ed consultant, after being in the industry for twenty-six years because it should change. So, I am going to start an educational reform movement that is considered rogue but necessary. I will do a lot of public speaking and writing." Definitively, that was not my answer.

In fact, to be called a female leader in the twenty-first century means you inevitably, invariably, almost certainly have had to push through exclusion, discrimination, verbal violence, and potential physical violence and have had to find something deep within yourself to overcome such challenges. Unabashedly, this book is about female leaders for young women leaders. Thus, while I normally would discuss how the human experience transcends the female experience, such a transcending, for this purpose, does not take place. And, if you are in the arena where you are considered a female leader in 2020, some s*** has gone down on the way to your rising up. No little girl wakes up and says, "I want to be a leader, Momma!" Please, let me imagine myself in positions where the scorched-earth policy of corporate management will lead me down paths where my very essence was questioned. Undoubtedly, if you are considered a woman leader in 2020, some s*** has gone down because just as sure as the sun will always rise, people along the way, in some places, will not bolster or support your success. Instead, their actions or lack of action will tear down your ambition, your courage, your strength by making you doubt your ideas and your voice, if not trying to snuff you out entirely. When I was a little girl, I never shouted from the rooftops, "I wanna be a leader!" The lone-wolf female leader is as powerful an archetype as the victim beaten down by life who can no longer go on and needs rescue. Despite it being almost 2021, these enlivened archetypes affect us on sub- and unconscious levels. What if there was a different way of perceiving how to understand the narrative of what happens to women on the path to leadership? What is certain is that along the way you will be asked to wear lots of masks and cultivate your persona to appear penultimately feminine—smart, but not too smart; bold, but not too bold; independent, but not singularly determined; a mix of Jessica Rabbit in a suit with a little sexy librarian sprinkled in—but do not be too effective or speak up if an idea is stolen from you or someone is speaking over you. Some things that happen on the path to being a leader will chip away at your soul, but that is the apparent path, so be steeled and resolute in fashioning a mask that one cannot see and that is easy enough of a persona to step into like a skin suit every day of the week.

Masks have had a moment in 2020. They are an emblem of survival and perseverance. Interestingly, the first spiritual psychologist in the west, Dr. Carl Jung (1875–1961), spoke of masks, personas, beauty, and the discovery of the personal, cultural, and collective shadow well over a century ago. Jung spoke of the hero's journey being nonlinear and unexpected, at once part of the collective and, also, uniquely personal. As is true to the convention of a resilience narrative, of a hero's journey, one will be looking for bits of what I overcame on the way to leadership to become the shining example of female self-actualized leader that I am supposed to be. What if, though, we were not the story, not made up of the story, but, instead, looked at the more compelling question, not of what happened, but instead to acknowledge that I know what happened *and* how do I get out of bed every day in spite of it? In the poem *Wild Geese*, Mary Oliver (1986) asserts the importance of owning the shadow, of exploring the larger macro- and smaller, heart-shaped micro-importance of the interpersonal and collective discovery of Self. Unapologetically, she provides advice to you, young female leader, that there is a place for you here:

> Whoever you are, no matter how lonely,
> The world offers itself to your imagination,
> Calls to you like the wild geese, harsh and exciting—
> over and over announcing your place
> in the family of things. (lines, 14–18)

It is in both the light of discovery and in the shadows of betrayal that answers the question, What is the story? or What happened on the path to being considered a female leader at the close of 2020? It is not a pinnacle event, not one singular point in time; it is universal and particular in that it is simply human. It is everybody's- and nobody's story.

There is a great misconception about leadership and life. Academia and its peripheral institutions have fashionably offered certificates, degrees, workshops, and courses that have monetized and created a "degree" for an inborn personality trait that is made up of a mix of charisma, intelligence, personality, and grit. I offer this from the perspective of being a specialty higher education consultant after twenty-six years of teaching, including fourteen years total in higher education leadership—specifically, a near-decade as the first female CEO of an innovative educational institution, having led it through a grueling accreditation process and, more importantly, a process of institutional discovery to become more mission-aligned and to serve students' Whole selves. It is in this role, as CEO, that, as an adult, I began hearing "You are a leader," "Look at how you lead," "You led well," and "You did a good job leading." The truth is that I followed my own instincts and passions, staying true to my true North while teaching and moved up through the ranks through administration over the course of my twenty-six-year career. Eventually, hard work gets recognized, and each level of management succeeded the one before until I reached the apex as a CEO. Then, in June 2019, at the decade mark, I decided to expand my reach as an educator, to consult with other organizations, and to speak publicly about a human-centered movement back to the heart for society, in general, but in the classroom, most particularly. That is the straight and simple answer as to how the path to leadership was made. There is a more complicated answer, though, worthy of exploration.

We cannot wish someone a leader, nor can the leader appoint him or her as such. It is a piece of our identity in which someone else states the claim "You are a leader." A true leader does not think of leadership while leading. The traits of a leader are inborn. Additionally, the environment also has a say in whether the traits that make up an emerging leader are polished, refined, and shiny, or snuffed out through—whether real or perceived—neglect, abandonment, and trauma. The sea change that has made leadership an industry assumes that we are in control of whether we have these inborn traits, and that, further, we have control over all aspects of our life's trajectory and story. For the most part, we are not in control of what happens to us in life. At the same time, we are not our tragedies, and we are certainly not the sole author of our triumphs.

We are in control of how we respond. The reality is that people who are considered resilient do not have a monopoly on saving themselves or being spared from life's unpredictable disappointments and tragedies. The one trait that determines if we become our story or can transcend it is *grit*. It is the one trait that is part of being a leader that people often do not talk about in the leadership industry because it is the *one* thing there is no way of capturing in a contrived academic lesson. You either have grit or you do not. Grit is the secret attribute that is the roaring underdog of leadership. Deconstructing leadership, as an umbrella term, reveals a combination of myth/archetype, narrative, perseverance, and grit.

Being a female leader in 2020 is to own your grit, your shadow, your truth. To look underneath the polished veneer of a successful female leader is to mine events like a scuba diver searching for treasure. It is at once to own that you have a place in history, in the books of myths and legends, but also to understand that it is an ever-evolving, living, breathing document. It is the narrative, the testimony, of self-discovery which is the literal fight for reclaiming the Self, after having emerged from the beautiful, mysterious wreck of Adrienne Rich's (1973) great metaphor and poem *Diving into the Wreck*. The story, your story, is a devastatingly beautiful relic within an intricate wreck from which we are supposed to emerge in a linear hero's journey. In a conventional story, one with conventional people, there would be an arc of personal and universal self-discovery. In the closing sixty days of the painfully human 2020, the path to leadership is more challenging to define, as we are ironically forced to lose the unconscious masks and personas, and, instead, place a literal mask on our face to live. To be an actualized and activated woman not willing to don the mask of outdated and outmoded archetypes is to acknowledge that while there is nothing new under the sun, the kaleidoscope of self, of soul, of the collective is the every-person challenge of this time. There is power in this time—it has changed, well, everything. It would be a crisis of leadership to fail to acknowledge the sheer power of watching an accomplished Black woman—ethnically diverse, with a foot in many worlds, who undoubtedly has had to wear many masks to get where she is and has amassed many stories—assert her agency in one simple phrase that every woman from whatever and every size, shape, and slice of life can relate: "Excuse me, Mr. Vice President, I am speaking." Every beating human heart on the planet who has skirted the margins of history, of the book of myths, has been talked over before. Courage is where the power of leadership lies. For women leaders, this moment requires a level of transparency to fully embrace what it looks like to be at the odd, uniquely quirky, and sometimes messy half-mark of life. In that 2020 moment of seeing clearly, Kamala Harris coalesced what it is to have grit. That is, the female leader's experience is one of having had to live through pain, discrimination, betrayal, and exclusion, as well as unprecedented support and opportunity, to remain a contender in the leadership arena; it is a mark of personal and collective struggle: "Mr. Vice President, I am speaking." That pioneering courage is the path to leadership. It is the path of truth and that thing that you cannot teach, convey, or pretend: grit.

To be sure, the answer to that question "What happened?" is important, sacred, and pedestrian. The more compelling answer is that despite all that did happen, how did you get up the next day, week, month, and year, to do it again, anyway? How did you not shrink back into self, and, instead, boldly reclaim your life from your story.

> It doesn't interest me. If the story you are telling me
> is true. I want to know if you can disappoint another

to be true to yourself. If you can bear the accusa-
tion of betrayal and not betray your own soul. If you
can be faithless and therefore trustworthy. I want to
know if you can live. I want to know if you can see
Beauty even when it is not pretty. Every day. **And if
you can Source your own life from its presence.**
(Oriah Mountain Dreamer, 1999, lines 41–55)

Source your own life from its presence, despite what has happened
in it. That is grit.

Thus, the question remains worthy of exploration and of this
sacred time when we have to wear masks in order to save our lives:
Jung's prophetic moment. Unmasking the leader is to discover that
her story is that everything happened that sometimes happens to
every woman and young girl, and nothing happened at all that was
extraordinarily, singularly mine.

Unmasking the self, the personas of industry, professionalism, and
convention, is to ascend and cultivate resilience, to save yourself:
"First having read the book of myths, and loaded the camera, and
checked the edge of the knife-blade, I put on the body armor of
black rubber" (Rich, 1973, lines 1–5). The female leaders' great
metaphor, the ladder, is always there to descend to the depths of
wisdom and ascend to transcend the noise in the everyday. The
ladder to save you, to climb up and out, or in this case, down to
uncover and discard, is right there innocently watching:

There is a ladder.
The ladder is always there
hanging innocently
close to the side of the schooner.

> We know what it is for,
> we who have used it.
> Otherwise
> it is a piece of maritime floss
> some sundry equipment (lines 13–21).

The ladder will always be there when you write your own rules and find your own mission statement. A warning to the female explorer: once you are there, do not forget, get complacent, and forget what you are there for:

> And now: it is easy to forget
> what I came for
> among so many who have always
> lived here
> swaying their crenellated fans
> between the reefs
> and besides
> you breathe differently down here (lines 13–21).

It is in the excavating of the soul, whether as a woman or as the collective non-androgynous integrated, nonbinary gently feeling Self in which Rich ends her treatise on the hero's journey. It is the every-story, at once every human and female story which requires a vulnerable courage to shake up the relics, the book of myths, the archetypes that no longer serve an evolved soul recognizing its humanness:

> I came to explore the wreck. The words are pur-
> poses. The words are maps. I came to see the dam-
> age that was done and the treasures that prevail.
> I stroke the beam of my lamp slowly along the flank

of something more permanent than fish or weed. **The thing I came for:** <u>the wreck and not the story of the wreck the thing itself and not the myth.</u> (my emphasis underscored; lines 57–63)

In donning the mask to save the self, the question of what happened is the story of everything and nothing. At once, it is a story of the existential despair of this mortal coil, and it is also a story of magic, mystery, and beauty: "'This is the place. And I am here,'" (lines 71–72), at once mermaid and merman.... "We circle silently about the wreck we dive into the hold. I am she: I am he" (lines 74–77). The path to leadership is its own greatest challenge: "We are the half-destroyed instruments that once held to a course the water-eaten log the fouled compass" (lines 83–86). It is in that spirit of the higher quest for meaning, of shedding false versions of the Self, that we, female leaders, find waiting a more powerful truth:

> We are, I am, you are
> by cowardice or courage
> the one[s] who find our way
> back to this scene carrying a knife, a camera
> a book of myths
> in which
> our names do not appear (lines 87–94).

To be a female leader is to acknowledge that while our names may never appear in the book of history, we will carry this time anyway, in spite of it; that is, grit.

Dear Young Female Leader, therein lies my advice: say what you mean and want what you want when you want, and then try to be silent again. It won't work. To be fully human is to realize that one is always on one side of history. But, that is still not the important story of now. The least compelling answer, personally, in what happened on my particular path to leadership is also ironic and revelatory in its timeliness. Logic would have it that the necessary follow-up question to my very nonlinear answer would then be to reveal what was the biggest obstacle on the path to leadership. Unequivocally, it was being a single working mother in the field of education and having taught and led in some form or another within the ranks of the surprisingly vicious, cut-throat industry— from the C-Suite of higher education from admin to professor to CEO to CxO-suite strategic consultant and writer. Early on, I wish that I had known before I least expected it that to be true to Self is sometimes to betray another. And, at the same time, it is also time to recognize the aggressions of institutions on us—whether healthcare, institutional, governmental, educational, financial, or interpersonal. If literature and new media are to be believed, to be a leader is to be true, courageous, and vulnerable to the calling. In its most traditional convention, the story of the female leader is the narrative outsider, skirting the book of myths, skating alongside its margins.

At the roaring end of 2020, grit is the story of female leadership. Our time now mimics Rich's Self metaphor of being at once uniquely human, extraordinary, and not particular to self or gender, but, instead, to be loyal to the beating of your heart, regardless of whether you will ever be included in the historic myths. We who know, know that there is another book; all that is written is written there. In that book, the intersection of history, culture, class, race, and gender is not the only option. In that narrative, exploring the wreck is what keeps us nimbly able to navigate it. Our grit, as female leaders, is to do what needs to be done in the day and to find beauty and fierce accomplishment in the apex historical moment of progress when an unapologetic professional Black female leader on prime-time American television can say, "Mr. Vice President, I am speaking."

In 2020, if we have lived through it, we have lived and possibly died by its vagaries. The hero's journey is not an arc, a bell curve, a linear line of heightened conflict and then the relief of integration. It is a nonlinear unfolding of events that are both and at once larger than the Self. At the closing of 2020, I am humbled by the answer to the question and by the idea that there is an answer at all—even more so, that the answer has been there all along. Young girls and women, my wish for you: let's envision the best of the best of the best for you. You, living your best life beyond what you think is imaginable; let's envision that beyond place and go beyond there together.

REFERENCES

Mountain Dreamer, O. (1999). *The Invitation*. Retrieved from http://www.oriahmountaindreamer.com/.

O'Connor, F. (1955). The Life You Save May Be Your Own. *The Complete Stories of Flannery O'Connor*. Farrar, Straus, & Giroux.

Oliver, M. (1986). *Wild Geese*. Retrieved from https://www.vanderbilt.edu/olli/class-materials/2017Summer.MindfulnessWk1.pdf.

Rich, A. (1973). *Diving Into the Wreck*. Retrieved from https://poets.org/poem/diving-wreck.

ABOUT DR. HOPE

Hope Phillips Umansky, PhD has spent the past twenty-six years holding different positions in independent and private institutions as faculty, administrator, academic dean, program director, Western Association of Schools and Colleges (WASC) accreditation liaison officer (ALO), and CEO. In June 2019, she was compelled to launch Innovations: Education Advocacy Group, Inc, a consulting practice in higher education management and leadership. EAG is distinct in that it creates fully individualized educational management initiatives and strategic plans, without the use of templates or "tried and true" initiatives. EAG is singularly student centered and mission aligned; that is the most robust and vigorous growth driver. Besides her consultant work, Dr. Hope does public speaking, writing, teaching, and consultant work. More on her consultant practice, Innovations: Education Advocacy Group, Inc., can be found at www.innovationsadvocacy.com

Dr. Hope has attended and worked at traditional and nontraditional schools and believes that education comes in many ways and forms. She holds a Bachelor of Arts in English literature from Scripps College; a Master of Arts in Liberal Studies, English literature, from Reed College; and master's and doctoral degrees in clinical psychology from California Institute for Human Science (CIHS), a boutique graduate institute. Her work at CIHS began in 2010 as associate dean, and each year, she was appointed with progressively increasing responsibilities as academic dean, WASC ALO, and CEO. For almost ten years, she led the institution through the WASC process and had unprecedented growth.

Innovations: EAG has a proprietary system for a total overhaul and culture realignment to re-engage students for organic and sustainable growth that is also fully mission aligned. Hope's passions within this work are engaging with students to incite their natural love of learning; conducting professional and faculty development, including creating strategic communication and holding gender, culture, and inclusivity trainings; spending time on campuses experiencing school culture at all levels; managing board communication and development; and engaging internal and external stakeholders in forward-thinking ways. EAG's fully customized plans are designed within the school's or organization's culture to create truly forefront internal and external initiatives. A singular focus on the student experience and mission alignment through all levels of the institution advances rigor and success while still honoring the whole student in the contemporary educational landscape.

BE QUIET, BE STILL, THEN ROAR!

Sarah Jean Sagredo-Hammond
President

SARAH'S PATH TO LEADERSHIP

My parents were migrant workers. My father joined the Air Force, and after he served his term, he and my mother, who had been high school sweethearts, came back to where they had grown up in the Rio Grande Valley and built their own home. My father began Atlas Electric and Air Conditioning. As a ten-year-old, I remember crying when my father would leave to go to work, begging him to let me work with him in the field of electrical contracting and air conditioning, and being told to stay home and help mom in the kitchen and around the house—that this industry was no place for me, a girl. Fast-forward to now: I am President of the company.

I started in 1997, working with my mom on finances and tax preparation. I moved into a full-time position in 2008. Learning from dispatching, filing, and invoicing, I created a structure for financing customers. I brought our accounts receivable from $600,000 down to $250,000 in four months. In 2011, my mother had a stroke and was left half paralyzed. My father decided he wanted to be her main caretaker and needed to step back from his role. Either we would have to close or one of us would have to step up and take the reins. I loved what I was doing: working in the office; running the teams; and hiring and running management, marketing, and finance. I had already gotten pretty involved in the community and affairs of our local area. I took on the role of President in 2012 and have loved every moment of it. I am passionate about our company because it was started with heart, integrity, and hard work! I remember the days when my parents did not pay themselves because they wanted to build the company and take care of the employees.

In 2014, we added refrigeration, and in 2016, plumbing. We have grown our small business and continue to want to bring change and be the one-stop solution for our customers and community. We also feel very strong about giving back. I know that the community needs so much support, as do our employees. So, we look for ways to help improve our employees' lives and support them in their home as well as support organizations in ways where we can truly make an impact on the ones in need. During COVID-19, Atlas started selling Fresh Air Apco X dual-light systems to protect families in their homes. But it was not enough to sell the product: we purchased it for all employees and installed it in their homes at no cost to them. This is an example of the role that Atlas and I will continue to support in the Rio Grande Valley.

SARAH'S GREATEST CHALLENGE

One of the greatest challenges in what has traditionally been a man's industry is changing the mindset of what a woman is capable of doing. I have had job applicants who decided not to work for the company because a woman was leading it. My technicians have been made fun of at vendor warehouses because they work for a woman. Customers have told me they want to speak to the man in charge. I have been asked numerous times what it is like working in a man's world. My answer to that is "Welcome to my world!" This is not a man's world; mine is a male-dominated industry, but you are speaking to me, and this world belongs to me. Ask me how I am doing; don't give my world to men. I truly believe that when a woman is able to understand herself, her triggers, and her growth points, and when she can admit when she needs to work on something, then she can truly find her voice and lead with that. I did not want to lead my company like a man—wearing jeans and button-down shirts has never been part of my daily wardrobe. I dress like a woman because that is what I have always liked and worn— dresses and heels—unless the occasion calls for steel-toe shoes and jeans to walk up a ladder.

I equate this world of mine to *Alice in Wonderland*, where the Caterpillar constantly asked Alice "Who are you?" She was troubled by that question. I challenge every woman to answer "Who are you" with grace and dignity and, most of all, with that inner voice that challenges what we were taught initially, to be quiet. Answer "Who are you?" with the roar of a lion!

I found my voice when I was able to leave a struggling relationship, in which my estranged husband, in an effort to make me stop the divorce proceedings, kidnapped me and abused me. I went missing for two days and lay handcuffed to the back seats of a truck, stripped naked and terrified. Prayer to Jehovah God saved me. When I was finally released and able to walk on my own, I learned that nothing could ever again stop me from speaking up. I found my lion's voice and turned her into a lioness. I shudder that any other woman would have to live an ordeal of so much trauma, and I now work hard to speak out to women in abusive relationships. Sometimes women stay in these because they have not understood their own voice or vision. Find yourself, be yourself, love yourself.

SARAH'S BEST ADVICE

I grew up seeing my mother do it all by herself, be a strong leader, run businesses, lead her family, and run them all without a woman next to her to provide support, without a woman to offer understanding, without a confidant. I could not understand why she wanted to cook in her heels after our church gathering; why she would not take care of herself. She never stopped to think about herself; she never gave herself priority; she lived for her children, Jehovah God, her husband, and her businesses. She never stopped to breathe and relax, and she was there for every friend who needed a listening ear. She preached and taught the Bible not only to her family, but to those in the community. She gave and gave and gave. I was cooking and cleaning and washing laundry by the age of eight and continued to help my mother while she worked and kept the balls up in the air doing her juggling act. I am most proud that by the age of five I had memorized all the books in the Bible and could sit and do bible study with others. My mother had taught me to read, and I was able to share in those teachings. Today she is paralyzed and needs the help of many to be mobile. She moved mountains—and still does with thoughts and words of wisdom—but she never cared for herself first.

I wish she had practiced more self-care. It's important to stop to enjoy and relax your heart and your mind. Practice whatever self-care you need to develop a strong sense of self and teach that to your children. I work all hours of the day, and I dedicate a lot of hours to the community, my children, and my husband, but I also make time for my self-care. I organize my calendar to be able to stop and breathe, and I hope to instill that in my staff: their own self-care. During COVID-19, I leaned in even more to the priorities of my head, my heart, and my needs and wants. The book *Eighteen Inches: The Distance Between the Heart and Mind* explains that how you live your life depends on those eighteen inches and what you do with them. I encourage you to find your self-care, your smile, your thoughts, and your quiet. The world taught women that we were to be quiet, so we struggle with finding our voice. Today I ask you to be quiet and to find your thoughts, but then roar with your voice, stand strong, stand kind, stand healthy.

ABOUT SARAH

Sarah Jean Sagredo-Hammond is the President of Atlas Electrical, Air Conditioning, Refrigeration & Plumbing Services, Inc., located in Alton, Texas. The family business has been in operation since January 1983. The company services extend from Laredo, Brownsville, and Corpus Christi up

to Austin. Today the business enjoys a 3,000-sq.-ft. facility, employees thirty-four, and has partnership service locations throughout the Rio Grande Valley. Sarah helped create an in-house financing market that provides clients with stronger financial positioning.

She holds a paralegal certificate and worked with an attorney for seventeen years, and she holds a finance degree and a real estate degree from Texas A&M University. She has been working on the accounting books for Atlas Electrical and Air Conditioning since she was fifteen and took over the financials in 1997. In 2012, she was made President. She has her own business, Financial Solutions; is a partner with Intentionally BridgeIt, an organization that spearheads women business owners; and is the manager for the Sagredo Rentals.

She also oversees management of Hummingbird Trailer Park, which is a winter Texan park for her family that is at maximum capacity every year. She further manages rental Alton X-Plex and other real estate and has invested in other entrepreneur ideas. Sarah maintains an active role in the community on behalf of Atlas and serves on several boards: She has previously served as Chair of SCI Women's Business Center and Chair of Organization of Women Executives. Currently she is President of Femfeshionals RGV and is a Collective Director 1 of 7 in the US for FemCity. She also serves as a board member for Women in HVACR, which is one of her strongest missions. Her passion is to help women grow businesses, and she speaks on this issue across several world and national platforms. She has served on several Texas boards and currently is a board member for the Greater Houston Better Business Bureau and South Texas Board. She also serves as an Advisory Board Member for the Rio Grande Valley Partnership, IB Grant Chair, and RGV Hispanic Chamber Small Business Development Chair along with several other committee organizations.

She was published in *100 Words/100 Women* by South Texas College and has been published in the McAllen Chamber Ad and *I am Latino Magazine*. She was also featured in the Special Edition of the *Amazons Watch Magazine* as one of the top twenty global women to watch in 2016. She has spoken on national platforms and at conferences as a guest speaker.

In December 2017, she graduated with a certificate in Scaling Business from Stanford University Graduate of School of Business. She was accepted to Leadership Texas 2020. In 2016, she was the recipient of the Women in Technology for South Texas College, and in 2018, she was chosen as the Mission Chambers Executive of the Year. She received the 2015 Global Champion for Women Economic Development Award in Dubai. She was inducted into the SAMEAWS 2015 Global Women Leaders Hall of Fame. She was named a South Texas College Women in Technology Advocate, in 2014 she received the Small Businessperson of the Year Award for the Rio Grande Valley, and in 2015, the RGV Hispanic Women of Distinction–Rising Star Award.

Although business and community involvement are important and part of her mission for her self-growth, what brings most happiness to Sarah is her family. She is married to Coach Marty Hammond, and together they have three strong daughters. She has lived in Alton, Texas most of her life and married her husband from Alabama who coaches arena football.

IMAGINE AND REIMAGINE A BETTER WORLD AND A BETTER LIFE

Lucy Sorretini
CEO, Impact Consulting LLC

LUCY'S PATH TO LEADERSHIP

My path to leadership started when I was a young girl, and it has been shaped ever since by my diverse experiences, unique circumstances, and broad perspectives growing up as a Latina in New York's inner city.

I was born and raised in the South Bronx as the daughter of two Puerto Rican parents from humble beginnings who emigrated from Puerto Rico to New York to fulfill their dream of providing a better life for themselves and their family. Quite typical, right? What is not so typical is what followed. Unfortunately, that dream came to a crashing halt when my father died unexpectedly in his early forties, leaving my mom a widow at the age of thirty-three to raise seven children, who were between the ages of nine months and seventeen years old, and a bodega (grocery) business to manage.

Unbeknownst to me, this is where my leadership journey would begin. As the youngest of the seven children, I do not have any early childhood memories of my father, but I do recall sadness and stillness whenever his name was mentioned in my presence. The general sentiment was that life had somehow been unfair to me and that my life would somehow be affected by this loss.

Thereafter, memories from my early childhood through early adulthood were filled with dichotomies and complexities that, while hard to describe, are common in communities of color, forcing affected young people to grow up and learn life and leadership lessons much too quickly.

On the surface and on a good day, my life was quite normal. It consisted of family visits: hanging out with friends; playing with my nieces and nephews; hours of watching television and playing with dolls; tagging along on my sisters' dates; working in my mom's grocery store; eating her delicious dinners; acting in house plays; going to school; planning our annual trip to Puerto Rico; volunteering in our neighborhood; attending church, political, and community events; and having discussions and debates with my stepfather.

On a bad day, my life was lonely, sad, somewhat disconnected, and—some might even suggest—dysfunctional. I realized that we were living in a neighborhood plagued by gun violence, drugs, incarceration, teen pregnancy, domestic abuse, and limited opportunities to break the cycle of poverty and social injustice. In some instances, these issues were much closer to home than I would have chosen to admit. So, as a young girl, I created my alternate experience, where I would imagine and reimagine a better world and a better life for myself, despite my circumstances. Some might call it coping; I call it visioning.

These experiences, both real and imagined, have shaped who I am as a person, how I show up as a leader, and how my leadership path has been influenced. I would not trade them for anything in the world, as they are foundational reminders of my leadership journey to date.

Life Is Fragile

Although I did not recognize it at the time, losing my dad as an infant would have me value life, recognizing that life can sometimes be way too short and incredibly fragile. From one moment to the next, life can turn from good to bad or vice-versa; in one instant, it can even cease to be. My dad's death taught me to appreciate those who are living and those who have come before to pave the way for where we are today. It equally taught me to value each moment and each person in my life, to do my best to not sweat the small stuff or hold grudges, and to show gratitude for the many experiences— some blessings and some not—recognizing that tomorrows are not guaranteed and that the only thing we have for certain is the present moment. It was at this early age that I made a choice to live my life as someone who had gained much more than she had lost, establishing a broader perspective and deep connection to the gift and fragility of life. Most importantly, this period taught me that while we might not be able to choose our circumstances, we can always choose our perspective and how we respond. Life, in essence, is what we make of it. Cliché but so true.

We Are Resilient

Thereafter, I witnessed sacrifice and consequence in its greatest form. I watched my mom, a young widow with seven children, lean into her new normal. She spent countless hours working in the grocery store to support our family. Her work ethic was exemplary, but it came at the expense of limited time at home with her children. While these would not be ideal circumstances for anyone, she managed to do the best she could to give us a good life, often relying on my older siblings and extended family members to pitch in as needed. It required many sacrifices and a daily balancing act, and while it was not perfect, she made it work. We all did.

At the time of this writing, I am much older than my mom was when she became widowed, but even so, I cannot fathom what that experience must have been like for her. Despite the unfortunate circumstance of my dad's passing, her limited resources, and her lack of business savvy, she managed to find the inner strength to carry on, in large part due to her strong faith. She raised our family and ran the family business in a way that makes me so proud even today—always focused on community and helping those who were worse off than us and always imparting the right balance of wisdom and tough love that would set straight anyone on a crooked path. And she always showed up with a humble heart and servant mindset, reminding us daily that with God's will, "si dios quieres"—all things are possible. Her memory is a living testament of what it means to be a person of faith and to be resilient, and it is the benchmark I use whenever I face challenging situations in my career, my business, and the rest of my life. She was, for certain, my very first role model and, by far, one of the strongest influences in my life.

Social Justice Matters

In my middle childhood years, the one thing I soon became aware of was how different the world in which I lived was from what I saw on television. With few exceptions, my family, community, and neighbors—mostly Latino and Black—did not resemble the characters I had come to know and love on television. The family structures and homes we lived in did not look the same either. Most of the families in our neighborhood were single-family households or families living with grandparents and extended family members, and most of us lived in apartment buildings, not houses. Most of my friends were just like me—latchkey kids who, for the most part, looked after themselves until their parents or extended family members got home from work, making for many long and lonely days.

The opportunities afforded us were few and far between. And yet, despite these realities, I still felt more blessed than most because I was part of a community that looked after one another, and despite our struggles, I could clearly see how far worse off other families were than we were. To me, it just did not make sense and did not seem fair that some people could lack so much while others had so much. Again, I was making a comparison between what I experienced in real life and what I watched on television. It was during this time that I recognized privilege and became curious about and committed to social justice, despite not knowing what it was called.

Mentors Are Powerful

Throughout my life, I have been blessed with amazing mentors, both within and outside of my family. These were people who breathed hope and promise into my heart and my mind each day and took time out of their hectic schedules and complex lives to tutor, mentor, and motivate me, sometimes without even knowing they were doing so. They saw something in me that I did not see in myself at the time, and as a result, I was exposed to a new world of possibilities and opportunities.

During this time, my perspective shifted from one of circumstance to one of possibility and I began to create a bigger vision for my life, even bigger than I had dreamed about as a child because I now had a broader perspective to consider. I had come to appreciate business, community and the diversity of the people that were in my life. I longed for a meaningful career of my own one day. One that included doing well for myself but also making a difference and doing well for others. Helping others that might not otherwise be able to help themselves and pushing past limiting beliefs and stereotypes to create meaningful change and equity in the world. This led me to a career in human resources and eventually pursue my passion for driving change through diversity, equity, and inclusion consulting.

My Leadership Role Today

As I reflect on my path to leadership and my role today, I am reminded that leadership is not a passive sport, nor is it entirely about titles, pay rates, authority, power, or always being in control.

Leadership is so much more than these things. It is about one's ability to influence others toward a common goal or purpose, one that has higher-level impact. It is about making the world a better place through our thoughts, words, and actions and being in service to others.

I realize that the leadership attributes I learned when I was a young girl serve as the foundation for who I am today, how I show up, and what I value most. The journey to my current position as CEO of my own firm was somewhat untraditional but destined to play out exactly as it has. In my case, I believe that my current leadership role found me, and not the other way around. After having spent over twenty years in corporate America doing great work for amazing companies in the human capital space, I chose to follow my heart and pursue a new role in entrepreneurship that would allow me to leverage my life and work experiences to create change and meaningful social impact in a way that levels the playing field for underrepresented groups in businesses and communities globally. It has been over five years since I started Impact Consulting LLC, and I still feel blessed to be doing what I love every day, changing hearts and minds and creating more inclusive workplace cultures. My life has come full circle, and I am forever grateful for my path to leadership.

My Career Trajectory from Toddlerhood to Adulthood

At the age of four, I had a paying job at my mom's grocery store. In charge of switching out the milk in the refrigerator twice per week, I was paid $1 a week and learned to value work and looked forward to my weekly paycheck.

I received working papers while in high school, at the age of four-teen, and have worked ever since in mostly customer service and human resource roles. It was during this time that I found my gift and passion in working with people, and I grew to love the inde-pendence that came with making and managing my own money.

As a young adult, I accepted my first full-time job in marketing, working for a Fortune 100 insurance company. The independence that came with working outside of our family business, the New York City vibe, and working in big business were my great loves of the time, but I longed to work more hands-on with people.

I spent approximately four years in insurance. Then I took an HR role on Wall Street, which came with great money and a nice title, but I did not like the hustle, the stress, or the "every man for him-self" attitude that came with being on Wall Street. It was during this time that I became keenly aware of the stark difference between Wall Street and Main Street, witnessing firsthand how money can sometimes change people—and not always for the better. This unequivocally was not my thing.

Thereafter, I accepted an HR position with a global management consulting firm and fully embraced and appreciated the multicul-tural and problem-solving aspects of my role. I traveled the world, meeting amazing people and learning so much about different cul-tures while I worked on major human capital and business initia-tives focused on organizational change. Without a doubt, I grew as a person and decided to build on my twenty-year career in consulting.

In 2016, I took all of what I love about business, community, and people and blended it to create my own business, Impact

Consulting LLC, which was born with a thought and vision that our communities and businesses should have leaders that represent the constituents they serve; that all people, especially those from underrepresented populations, should have access to leadership opportunities; and that young people should see role models in top positions who look like them. As a company, our focus is on creating inclusive workplace cultures. This, by far, has been my best career move ever. Also, I joined the Board of Directors of Columbia Bank in New Jersey, an organization focused on supporting community businesses to grow and thrive.

LUCY'S GREATEST CHALLENGE

One of the greatest challenges I have had as a leader is managing and balancing my work and personal life, especially during those years when I was a single parent and my sons were younger. One thing I have learned about business is that it is not naturally suited to support the working parent. Despite affirmative action, equal employment opportunity, and other labor laws in place to support men and women in the workplace, company practices are still not fully supportive of the working parent. Since most women are also primary caregivers, being a businesswoman puts an undue burden on us and our families, leaving us at a major disadvantage. There is a general sentiment—or shall I say implicit bias—out there that says that when faced with the choice between business and family, women will choose family. And while I do not disagree, I wonder why it is that companies frown upon any individual prioritizing family over business. This, in my humble opinion, is something that should be rewarded and accounted for when setting up business rules of engagement. It is one of the core tenets to ensure that diverse populations remain in the workforce and progress to leadership positions. Never should anyone have to choose, as my mother did, between business and family. We should look for ways to enable both to co-exist, and yet, as we all know, they do not. I also find it quite interesting that the biggest challenge I faced as a leader was also my mom's biggest challenge, more than three decades prior.

I have dealt with this issue throughout most of my adult life, and it continues to be a work in progress for me despite my sons being of college age now. How I have dealt with it has varied, depending on my life and career stage and the age of my children at the time. Three main things come to mind:

1. **Establish clear expectations and rules of engagement.** I have found that when there are clear expectations around what the requirements of the role are, what is expected of me, and what I can realistically provide, it usually results in a win/win for me and the organizations I have worked with. This also holds true in my own business, when I am establishing expectations and rules of engagement with clients and employees. In some cases, I have found that there is not a fit between where I am and what I need and where they are and what they need, which is perfectly fine, but in most cases, we find a way to meet in the middle. It usually involves some level of negotiation to get to a place where both parties are comfortable and in agreement.

2. **Create space for open, honest, and timely dialogue.** Even with clear expectations and established rules of engagement, it is inevitable that situations will arise when we must change the plan or course of action. This has come up for me multiple times, and usually it is around a major life event. In my case, three such events come to mind:

(1) getting a divorce and needing to take a pause to determine how best to manage life as a single mom, (2) taking time off to care for my own mom prior to her dying from cancer, and (3) needing to put everything on hold to prioritize time with a son who just needs his mom's undivided attention. These are all real-life situations that many of us will inevitably go through in our lifetime; there is no rule that says we must go through it alone, so how I have chosen to deal with these situations is in being open and honest about what is going on in that moment and keeping my network and stakeholders informed.

3. **Consider options and create alternate plans.** The one thing I have learned about life is that it is full of surprises and unexpected events—some good, some not, some that are within our control, and others that are outside of our control. And while I cannot guarantee an alternate plan will save the day every time, not having a Plan B—or Plan C, for that matter—is a sure way to fail, disappointing yourself and possibly others. And so, to the best of my abilities, I always consider alternatives and options. Remember, I am that same little girl whose dad died unexpectedly when she was a baby—the girl who witnessed her mom and siblings struggle to adapt to and survive their new normal and who watched her stable structure drop from beneath her very tiny feet with no safety net nor a plan in place to pick up the pieces. And so, I have always felt compelled to create alternate plans for myself, keeping three very important things in mind: first, the fact that God is always in control; second, that when one door closes, it is usually because there is another door waiting to be opened; and third, believing that what does not kill us will only makes us stronger.

LUCY'S BEST ADVICE

My best advice for you, as a woman in a leadership role or one ascending into a leadership role, is three-fold. First, I would suggest that you have a vision for what type of leader you would like to be and understand why this is important to you. Having a clear understanding of what it means to be a great leader for yourself personally and in the context of your role and the organization you are employed by or the company you represent is critical.

Leadership is one of those broad terms that means different things to different people and the definition may vary by context, role and/or organization; therefore, ensuring alignment up front is critically important for success. One of the definitions of leadership is the ability to direct oneself, influence others toward a common goal, role model expected behaviors, and leverage strengths so everyone feels fulfilled and valued. This definition is a tall order by most accounts and so obtaining clarity and alignment is key for anyone in or ascending into a leadership role.

Second, if you are not already aware, I would also suggest you engage stakeholders to understand what matters most to them and assess how others view you in the context of this agreed upon and aligned definition of leadership. The voice of stakeholders is critical and helps in providing clarity on one's leadership brand, including strengths and gaps. This is a gift that cannot be underestimated and is often overlooked. The request for feedback lets stakeholders know that their perspectives matter and that part of your success is contingent upon how you show up for them.

Third, I suggest that you identify what your core strengths are and determine how best to leverage them in a way that feels natural and authentic, and delivers maximum impact and contribution to the organization and the stakeholders they serve because, at the end of the day, real leadership is about having impact and leveraging strengths so that everyone feels valued and fulfilled.

ABOUT LUCY

Lucy Sorrentini is the Founder and CEO of Impact Consulting, LLC, a certified minority- and woman-owned Management Consulting Firm with expertise in Talent and Organizational Development, Diversity, Equity, and Inclusion Consulting, Professional and Leadership Development Training, and Executive Coaching. Lucy is also on the Board of Directors of Columbia Bank and Columbia Financial Inc., in New Jersey.

Lucy has over twenty years of professional experience as a Strategy Consultant, Human Resources Leader, and Executive Coach at Fortune 1000 companies, such as Merrill Lynch, McKinsey & Company, and Booz Allen Hamilton, where she served as the Chief Diversity Officer and a Member of the HR Executive Team. Lucy is a trusted advisor, thought leader and business partner to organizations that want to attract, develop, engage, reward, and retain a diverse workforce, and align business and talent strategies to increase inclusion and unlock innovation. She is highly regarded by her clients and best known for her strategic business acumen, subject-matter expertise, collaborative and authentic leadership style, and results-driven approach to accelerate positive, high-energy, sustainable change.

Lucy earned her Executive MBA from Fairleigh Dickinson University and became a Certified Professional Coach by the International Coach Federation. She has also earned the distinction of Energy Leadership™ Master Practitioner from the Institute for Professional Excellence in Coaching, and she has a Myers-Briggs, MBTI® Certification. Additionally, Lucy completed the Kotter Change Management Strategy Certificate Program, and she is CQ and Unconscious Bias Certified by the Cultural Intelligence Center.

Lucy's affiliations include her HR Committee membership with the Commerce and Industry Association of New Jersey. She is an alumna of the Goldman Sachs 10,000 Small Business Program. Lucy also serves as the Chair of the Latina Philanthropy Circle of the New York Women's Foundation and is a Strategy Advisor and former National Board Member of Girls Incorporated. Lucy is a President's Council Member of The Acceleration Project (TAP) and volunteers at the Oasis New Jersey Haven for Women and Children.

PART TWO

NEVER STAY IN A PLACE
WHERE NO ONE SEES YOUR VALUE

Danielle Hansen
Director of Global Strategic Sourcing at Coloplast,
Professor, and President of Strategic Training Endeavors

DANIELLE'S PATH TO LEADERSHIP

Imagine you are in a forest. There is a path that is cut for you and another that is overgrown. Which one do you choose? I have continued throughout the course of my life to choose the path that is the most difficult. I am heavily motivated by challenging opportunities, and if someone tells me that I cannot achieve something, I have the drive and perseverance to show that I will. As an undergraduate at the University of St. Thomas, I obtained a triple major in operations management, legal studies in business, and Spanish in four years while working fifty hours a week. While most people were focused on your typical college experience, my existence was quite different.

Having graduated at the time of Enron scandals, it was extremely important for me to work with a company that was heavily rooted in their mission. Upon graduation, I took an internship with Medtronic, which has always had an extremely strong mission and values by which the company is governed. The position was supposed to have tactical buying responsibility, but due to my degrees and my passion for contracts, I was quickly provided a sink-or-swim situation where I was negotiating multimillion-dollar contracts internationally and developing the category strategy. It gave me the opportunity as an intern to find my passion for negotiation. While there, I completed my MBA with a focus in international marketing, obtained my Green Belt in Lean and Six Sigma, was Co-Chair of the Medtronic Twin Cities Community Council Leadership Cabinet and Membership Committee Chair of the Women's Council, and had my daughter. My focus during the first six years of my career was to ensure that I was obtaining knowledge while also stretching leadership through volunteer activities as well as employee resource group (ERG) participation. These two avenues provided me with additional leadership experience that I was not getting in my early roles.

After working in two different divisions and three different roles with increasing responsibility while at Medtronic, I decided to accept a position with Honeywell. At that time, Medtronic trained a significant amount of people on Lean and Six Sigma, but employing it into the culture had not gained much traction. Early in my career, I wanted to work with a company that lived and breathed Lean and Six Sigma to really apply the learnings from the program.

Honeywell provided a significant shift from the culture that I had grown accustomed to at Medtronic. I was able to take on increased responsibility, refine my negotiation skills, and manage higher-spend suppliers. It also provided me the ability to work in a truly global company, where on any given day I was meeting with Europe, Asia, and Central America. I continued to drive to achieve the key performance indicators (KPIs) that I was measured on and seek out additional opportunities through stretch assignments to drive productivity gains. At around my eighteen-month mark with Honeywell, some of the strategy shifted and the category management responsibilities were offshored. While I was spared the first wave of downsizing, the writing was on the wall, as my suppliers were in Asia and Mexico. As this was the first layoff that I had ever experienced, there were a lot of emotions and anxiety. Many of the people displaced had been with the company for 20+ years and had never needed a résumé or to look externally. I quickly stepped up to help people navigate LinkedIn, create résumés, etc. During this time, a past colleague of mine at Medtronic reached out to me for an opportunity at St. Jude Medical, another medical device company.

I was excited to get back into medical devices, as I am passionate about saving and improving people's lives. In this role, I had an opportunity to work for a different med-tech company, where I could apply the additional learnings from Lean and Six Sigma. In addition, I now had experience at a company that was much more mature in their strategic-sourcing life cycle. It gave me the opportunity to see what "best in class" looked like and understand what can and cannot work in a less mature model. While in this role, I took on the mentoring of supply management professionals in our emerging manufacturing locations, including Costa Rica and Puerto Rico, in an attempt to build my people-management skills. At this time in my career, I was had only been in cardiovascular device technology and wanted to have the opportunity to work for a company in a different medical device field.

I also found a need at this point in my career to invest in myself. I had reached a roadblock with my boss, who was unwilling to invest in development opportunities when I found it necessary to take a negotiation course. I asked for approval, but after making a formal presentation on the benefits to company that I could derive from having taken the course, I was denied funding. My boss told me that he would purchase me a book on negotiation but that I was not allowed to attend the course and he would not fund it. To anyone who negotiates, a book on negotiation is not a replacement to practicing negotiation techniques, as you would in a class. I took vacation time and self-funded my training at Harvard Law School's Program on Negotiation (PON).

Shortly thereafter, I took on a new role with Stryker. The position with Stryker allowed me to work in a different geography, California, while managing a supply base in Europe, Asia, and Central America. Here I was able to focus on finalizing my Black Belt in Lean and Six Sigma while also utilizing the courses that I had self-funded to develop and lead cross-functional communication and negotiation training. Throughout my time with Stryker, I took on an additional role and worked across divisions from a corporate perspective. I also started teaching in the MBA and Executive Education programs at the University of St. Thomas, which allowed me to teach others the life skill of negotiation. Teaching at University of St. Thomas also helped launch the founding of Strategic Training Endeavors, a woman-owned training and consulting company focused on providing expertise to close skill gaps and imparities throughout the workforce while retaining talent in an inclusive environment.

After having worked at Stryker for almost three years, traveling upwards of 90% of the time, I needed to focus on an opportunity that allowed me to move into a people-management role with less travel. I took on an opportunity with CPC (a subsidiary of Dover), which allowed me to work for a smaller company. It provided me the opportunity to develop, from the ground up, the strategic-sourcing organization within CPC while transforming the supply chain from an industrial-based company to a life sciences company. In addition, I had the opportunity to develop sourcing, working with tooling engineers/managers, interns, and rotational development professionals across CPC and Dover in the United States and China.

As a Director of Global Strategic Sourcing at Coloplast, I currently have the opportunity of leading the Global Strategic Sourcing Group in the United States and France, managing suppliers across the globe and developing and implementing the strategic vision. In addition, my role has provided me the opportunity to develop, from ground zero, the Coloplast Women's Council.

With each step in my career, I have consistently looked at (1) the value I bring to the organization and (2) the value the organization brings to my development. I want to ensure that with each step I take within an organization on my leadership journey I am making an impact and ensuring the organization gains from my expertise, leadership, and perseverance.

DANIELLE'S GREATEST CHALLENGE

One of the largest challenges that I've faced as a leader came in 2018 after being nominated by seven of my mentees for the Women's

Health Leadership TRUST Mentor of the Year Award. A week after I accepted the award, I received a message from a woman at my company. Her email provided me an opportunity to address a challenge that she was posing. This challenge was one that most companies find themselves navigating across various maturity cycles. She asked me directly what I was going to do to mentor women at this company. Her question that morning—"What are you going to do?"—continued to resonate with me throughout the course of my day.

That afternoon, I responded to her email. Having only been at the company for a few months, I had not had the opportunity to fully understand what was currently offered in the way of mentoring. However, I did respond that I would work to understand experiences and opportunities, and diligently work to transform development opportunities for women in leadership. After doing more due diligence and understanding additional people's wants and needs, I started lobbying for Employee Resource Groups (ERGs). Having worked at several companies with mature ERG programs, I understood the impact that these groups could have on their members. Reflecting on my own career journey, it was a great opportunity for me to obtain additional leadership roles and responsibilities at a quicker pace than my earlier roles had permitted.

As many people had never experienced ERGs, I was on a journey to educate and articulate the benefits to both the employees and the company. I continued to find additional platforms and people who would listen to the value proposition that ERG would bring to the company. It was my perseverance and passion for continuous improvement and people development that gained me approval within the organization. That day, I could hardly get the smile off my face! I knew that I needed to not only establish the Women's

Council but also to quickly set up a structured approval process for subsequent ERGs to follow.

What I did not know at the time was I would quickly be met with my next challenge. For this group to be successful I needed a full governance structure, mission, vision, values, benefits, KPIs, etc. These all needed to be pulled together quickly. I put out a call to employees in the organization, explaining the benefits of an ERG and adding a call to action for people who were interested in helping launch the first ERG. When that message was sent, I was anticipating having maybe five people agree to help. Instead, I was met with the next largest challenge: fifty people (both female and male) agreed to help launch this ERG. The excitement was shared, but how do you effectively ramp up from ground zero to a team of fifty? In those early months, there were a lot of good lessons learned around delegation and maintaining engagement across such a large team. Establishing additional leaders who could run each of the different committees soon became key as we continued to trailblaze.

Shortly thereafter, COVID-19 hit. As a trailblazing grassroots organization, we were faced with the need to transform to fit the new normal. People were now thrown into an environment of uncertainty and anxiety as their worlds shifted drastically. I pushed leadership of the committees to continue driving programs, expanding the membership base, and increasing our communications. We continued to migrate speaking sessions to online, hold virtual speed-networking sessions (allowing those who were missing contact with others to have a forum to expand their network), develop roundtable discussions, and launch a formal mentoring program. With the continued offerings, we were able to exponentially increase our membership—all at a time when employees were looking for more connection.

Looking back over the course of this journey, I never would have guessed that I would experience this opportunity or the global pandemic that hit. However, looking back, it is the fact that I and the Women's Council leadership team never halted our journey, despite the challenges and a global pandemic that make all this worthwhile. Looking back on the leadership challenge and knowing that we have persevered, seeing how the leadership team has further enhanced its leadership skills, and hearing from employees about the value that this ERG has brought to their lives makes me extremely proud of the success that we have achieved. None of this would have been possible without these four pillars: (1) know your value, (2) step up to negotiate, (3) exercise perseverance and resilience, and (4) understand the perception that you create with your actions.

DANILLE'S BEST ADVICE

My advice for women ascending into leadership would be to follow the four pillars listed above and discussed below.

1. Know Your Value

As a woman, you need to understand the value that you bring to the table. How do you differentiate yourself, your credentials, expertise, and leadership? Taking time to reflect and understand those strengths and differentiators that you possess will assist in shaping not only your value proposition but the confidence behind that value. This value is shown by the following story:

A father said to his daughter, "You graduated with honors. Here is a car I acquired many years ago. It is several years old. But before

I give it to you, take it to the used-car lot downtown and tell them I want to sell it. Then see how much they offer you."

The daughter went to the used-car lot, returned to her father, and said, "They offered me $1,000 because it looks very worn out." The father said, "Take it to the pawn shop."

The daughter went to the pawn shop, returned to her father, and said, "The pawn shop offered $100 because it was a very old car." The father said, "Take it to the club."

The daughter took the car to the club, returned, and told her father, "Some people in the club offered $100,000 for it since it's a Nissan Skyline R34, an iconic car that is sought after by many."

The father said to his daughter, "The right place values you the right way. If you are not valued, do not be angry; it means you are in the wrong place. Those who know your value are those who appreciate you. Never stay in a place where no one sees your value."

This story exemplifies the importance of understanding your value. It is a crucial first step in the journey to become leaders.

2. Step Up to Negotiate

Do not be afraid to negotiate. Too often I see women avoid negotiations altogether because they do not know their own value, lack self-confidence, and/or have been conditioned to think that their value is much lower than others'. One of the worst things that we as women can do is to step away from a negotiation. Negotiations do not have to be scary. They are a dialogue between two or more people or parties where a conflict exists. Whether it is a negotiation over employment, budget, resources, etc., it is an extremely important skill for women to develop. As women, we are problem solvers. We need to utilize this skill set to ensure we are maximizing the value we obtain in each negotiation we encounter. One of the quotes by Nora Roberts that resonates with me is, "If you don't go after what you want, you'll never have it. If you don't ask, the answer is always 'no.' If you don't step forward, you're always in the same place." This leads me to the third pillar.

3. Exercise Perseverance and Resilience

As you ascend to leadership roles, there will be many barriers encountered throughout your journey. You will not be able to drive change and transformation without quickly learning perseverance. Perseverance is "persistence in doing something despite difficulty or delay in achieving success." Resilience is "an ability to recover from or adjust easily to misfortune or change." Change is a difficult thing for most people to encounter. As you ascend to leadership, you will find yourself in situations where you need to persist despite the opposition and barriers in front of you. You will want to be resilient so when you are knocked down, you are able to get back up and continue.

There are many times where your idea is new to the organization, and due to the uncharted newness, many people will erect mountains of barriers and discourage your perseverance. It is easier to be pushed off course than to continue exercising persistence and resilience, but if we allow our course to be shifted, the gains will be nonexistent. If we do not persevere, we will not achieve greatness.

4. Understand the Perception that You Create with Your Actions

The fourth pillar is perception. Maya Angelou stated, "I've learned that people will forget what you said, people will forget what you did, but people will never forget how you made them feel." So often, we think about leadership in terms of the concrete skills that it takes to be a leader, often overlooking the also important soft skills. Understand that each encounter with a person is an opportunity to either build up or tear down the relationship. As you embark on your leadership journey, know the perception that you are leaving with each encounter.

ABOUT DANIELLE

Danielle Hansen is Director of Global Strategic Sourcing at Coloplast and the President and Founder of the first Coloplast ERG, the Coloplast Women's Council.

She serves as an Adjunct Professor at the University of St. Thomas and the University of Minnesota, teaching negotiation strategy in UST's MBA and executive education programs and Supply Chain and Operations Management in UM's Carlson School of Management. In addition, Danielle is the Founder and President of Strategic Training Endeavors, a woman-owned training and consulting company focused on providing expertise to close skill gaps and imparities throughout the workforce while retaining talent in an inclusive environment.

She possesses an extensive background in international supplier relationship management, contract manufacturing, negotiation, project management, and continuous improvement. She graduated cum laude with a triple major in legal studies in business, Spanish, and operations management in 2004 from the University of St. Thomas. In 2009, she completed her MBA with a focus in international marketing, also from the University of St. Thomas. She attended three executive education courses at Harvard Law School, including International Business Negotiations, Leadership and Negotiation, and Advanced Master Negotiator in 2013. In addition, she is certified as a Lean and Six Sigma Black Belt (LSSBB) and a Certified Professional in Supply Management. Throughout her tenure, she has earned numerous awards, including the 2018 Mentor of the Year Award, Six Star Financial Results Award, Employee of the Month, People's Choice Award, and a Collaborative Inquiry Research grant. Danielle continues to train on topics of negotiation, risk mitigation, contract management, continuous improvement, supplier communication, conflict management, emotional intelligence, and strategy.

Danielle is passionate about improving people's lives and has had the opportunity for the past sixteen years to impact/improve people's lives on a daily basis through ensuring continuity of quality supply of medical device, biopharmaceutical, and industrial products while at Coloplast, CPC, Stryker, St. Jude Medical, Honeywell, and Medtronic.

In addition, Danielle is passionate about developing future leaders. She mentors your purpose, not just your person. She is gifted at seeing the potential in you far before you see it in yourself. She takes the time to understand the challenges each of us faces, regardless of our race, gender, or age—she sees through a nonjudgmental lens, embracing and welcoming diversity, as if to say, "Come to the table; there's room and a need for all of us here."

WHEN YOU PLAY SMALL, YOU'RE NOT SERVING THE WORLD

Jackie Stallings Evans
CEO, Solutions Strategist, Leadership Coach,
Consultant, Speaker, and Author

JACKIE'S PATH TO LEADERSHIP

My path to leadership started while working at IBM Corporation in sales. Although many know that IBM has been a leader in technological advancement, few may know that IBM was also a leader in its commitment to equal opportunity long before affirmative action. As a result, after the Civil Rights Act of 1964 was passed, IBM stepped up its recruitment to hire more Black Americans.

I was one of those individuals, the first generation in my family to work in corporate America and one of those protesters taking a stand for civil rights. However, I did not realize what a pivotal step this was for me to work for a Fortune 50 company. The only thing that mattered to me at that time was that we, as Black Americans, would finally be given the opportunity to demonstrate our value. After all, this was what we had been protesting decades for: to be judged by the content of our character and not by the color of our skin. It was time!

It is so hard to believe that it has been over thirty-five years since I first walked into IBM. I remember that day as if it were yesterday. There was absolutely no one who looked like me. This was not, however, an unfamiliar scene. In fact, my new corporate environment looked a lot like my high school environment. I was Black and a woman. I was once again thrust into an environment unknown to my race and culture. In my culture, we were raised to believe that if we worked hard, we would excel, achieve, and be acknowledged for our good deeds. Nothing could have been further from the truth in this competitive, corporate, cutthroat sales environment.

IBM was in its growth life cycle, setting industry standards and growing market share. If you watched the movie *Hidden Figures*, you might recall how huge the IBM mainframes were during NASA's preparation to land its first man on the moon. These machines were IBM's cash cow. Interestingly, these machines were flying off the shelves. Just selling one of these mainframes was all a sales representative needed to reach one's yearly quota! They were easy to sell but hard to install and even harder to keep in. So, the sales representatives were overly aggressive to make sure that they got the best technical sales representatives assigned to their accounts.

As a new employee, I worked alongside a talented technical sales representative, Celeste, who was well respected and in demand. So, I got to learn from one of the best. But how did I get assigned to her? It was a blessing! The first thing that Celeste told me was that I had the skills and was much further along than I thought: "You just have to be more confident and continue to grow your skills. You got this!" She told me to think about how I could be "the best rep." Not *good*, but the *best*! What did I need to do to be recognized by my peers as being the best? I studied fanatically to develop those skills. Celeste's business insights were true. Her words helped me to focus on what mattered in my new corporate culture: building my personal brand and expertise.

In addition to the above, building and leveraging relationships was important in sales. So, I would go out for drinks after work or grab a marketing representative and invite him to lunch. I write "him" since most of the sales representatives were white males. I focused on listening and began to build relationships. In the corporate world, after-hours networking is as essential as your 9-to-5 role. What I learned was that in settings outside the work environment, people tend to loosen up. You find out more about who they are, their families, and what is important to them. These meetings also gave them an opportunity to get to know me better. There were times that I had to be a gopher: make copies, make their presentations, and drop off materials to their clients. The more I complained about it to my peers, the more they told me that I had to pay my dues, just like everybody else. Then I remembered what my dad, the late Rev. R. W. Stallings, would say each Sunday as he closed his sermon. "When you come to a mountain and you can't go through it, look to your right, look to your left, look over it, look under it. There is a WAY...around the mountain."

So, I began to look at this gopher hassle as an opportunity. Each time I dropped off materials to clients, I would use it as an opportunity to introduce myself and let them know that I was a part of the sales team, working to ensure that they got what they needed to have a successful installation. Once the sales representatives knew that they could depend on me, they involved me even more. As such, I offered to read their proposals and identified things to include in their proposals so they would be more competitive. I realized the power of honing my expertise.

Each month, the management team recognized the sales and technical sales representatives, leaving me shocked and confused as to why I was never mentioned. Nonetheless, I congratulated those who were recognized and began to talk to them to learn more about what they did to get the recognition. Throughout those discussions, a message hit me repeatedly, that they were promoting themselves. As I stated earlier, I was taught not to boast. Just do your job and your good work will be recognized. How could I boast and remain true to myself? I needed a plan where my clients and team members would willingly acknowledge my contributions.

Prior to each customer installation, I decided to ask my clients about their expectations to ensure that they viewed our job as essential to a successful installation for their company. A checklist was created for what they wanted. At the completion of the installation, I would sit down with them to review the checklist. If they were happy, I would ask them to share their feedback with my management team. I even offered to draft a letter for them since I knew they had a busy schedule. Most of the time, they said, "Yes, please do." This gave me an opportunity to include all the things that I did to ensure a satisfied client. Moreover, I was able to leverage my happy clients to share my good work and expertise with my management team. This turned out to be a winning strategy.

After a couple of years, it became apparent that I needed to gain a better understanding of the business. I decided to go back to school to earn my MBA. Developing business acumen enabled me to look at the "big picture" and make recommendations to help move the business forward to achieve our corporate goals. I realized that when I was able to meet or exceed our goals, both the company and I win. Having that strategic view was a game changer.

As such, investing in myself, networking, immersing myself into the IBM culture, and exceeding expectations were instrumental in helping me to get promoted into my first leadership role of managing people. I was a good individual contributor. But I quickly learned what Marshall Goldsmith writes in his book *What Got You Here Won't Get You There*: the skills to be a great individual contributor are not the same skills needed to be an effective leader.

What were these skills that I needed? I did not know. But I knew two things:

1. I was given one of the largest teams in the office and the largest sales quota, with the responsibility of managing the team's revenue and expenses while achieving profit. I was overwhelmed! To succeed, I had to manage the business flawlessly. My business acumen skills were really going to be tested.

2. I was not going to run my business with the same command-and-control leadership style that so many of my managers used. I did not think it was an effective style.

So, I committed to lead in a way that would motivate the team to produce results. I knew then and now that people perform if they trust you and believe you care.

In light of the above, I came into this new job with a three-step plan.

Step 1: I scheduled meetings with each of my peer managers in the office. This approach helped me to begin to build relationships while getting the "real deal" on what was going on in the office. A few questions that I asked them were as follows:

- What were two to three soft skills most needed to do their jobs?

- What worked for them?

- What would they do differently?

- What would they suggest I do during my first ninety days on the job?

I learned that some of the "soft skills" that I needed to focus on were listening, effective communication, decision making, problem solving, and critical thinking.

Step 2: I met with everyone on my team on an individual basis to get their view of what was happening in the office. I only listened. It was important to understand their needs and wants so that I would know how to best manage and leverage the team. I gained clarity on each team member's skill set. "Meeting them where they are" and growing them from that point proved to be a valuable approach. These conversations helped me to identify the subject-matter experts, team leads, and mentors in the group. I now knew how to best utilize the different skills in the group.

Step 3: I scheduled a team-planning session with the purpose of reviewing the current state of our business and to lay out a well-defined business plan to achieve quota. At the end of our planning session, everyone knew what was expected as well as their roles to play that would help the team achieve quota. During this time, our competitors were competing for our accounts and displacing equipment. We had to secure our equipment. Our strategy was to check in more frequently with our clients to ensure that they were happy and had no concerns.

One of the biggest challenges I faced was recognizing individuals and teams. I could give small branch awards (up to $2,500) without upper-level management approval. However, if I wanted to give a director's award (up to $5,000) or headquarters award (up to $10,000), I had to compete with my peer managers. These were distinguished awards, and approval was hard to get. Headquarters would approve only so many of these awards each month. Because I did not understand how to navigate through the organization and play the political game, my people were losing out on recognition, despite performing at the top of their game and helping to close deals. Morale was low, and this was by far my hardest leadership challenge.

What did I need to do to get my team recognized?

I knew that I had to step outside my office and meet the decision-makers in the region and at headquarters. So, every time I would go to the region (New York City) or headquarters (Armonk,

New York), I scheduled a meeting to update them on what was going on in the local office.

I also decided to draft a template for the team to use, including their accomplishments; a letter from their client; and feedback from anybody else in the office that they worked with. I encouraged them to join any meetings that the sales representative had with their manager or the installation team and to play a lead role in those discussions. This gave them more visibility and really helped me to bring a stronger case to solidify the director and headquarters awards. I was seen in the region and headquarters as a manager who got results. This positioned me for my next move to the region as a regional support manager in New York City.

My team was responsible for providing second-level technical support to the northeast tri-state area (New York, New Jersey, and Connecticut offices). Two years later, I was promoted to headquarters as the global learning leader responsible for providing internal and external training for clients using IBM's midrange products. I was growing and becoming more and more confident in my abilities as a leader. This is why it is so important for companies to step up and provide mentors and sponsors to *all* candidates who show potential—regardless of race or gender. Can you imagine what I could have achieved with the right support system?

After leaving IBM, I founded a leadership model and company called What Do You Do When Leadership, Inc, a minority and woman-owned management consulting, leadership development, coaching, and training firm headquartered in Atlanta, Georgia. We work with high performers and high-potential leaders to take them to their next level of leadership. I am finally in my sweet spot where

I work with clients to help them "up" their game. This has truly been a rewarding experience!

I have always wondered why God chose a little Black girl from the deep segregated South to go down this leadership path. My journey took me from being an entry-level programmer to an executive at a Fortune 50 company. This was not easy. Most of the time, I did not have mentors or sponsors to guide me. I now know that God chose this journey for me. My purpose was and has always been to reach back and help others. "To whom much is given, much will be required" (Luke 12:48). Each job helped me to become a more effective leader and learn the political strategies required for success in corporate America. What an exciting leadership journey this has been!

JACKIE'S GREATEST CHALLENGE

My greatest challenge in the corporate space has been to gain the respect and support of my peers, as I was stereotyped. Often, their first impression was that I was "in the room" only because I met HR's diversity criteria—being Black and a woman. However, once they got to know me, they realized that I was knowledgeable, provided value, and was an asset to the team.

When I walked down those halls at IBM's headquarters, all you would see were six-foot-tall white men with blond hair who ran the company. I was 5'2" and a woman of color. So, the greatest challenge for me was being respected as a leader. My peers recognized that I knew what I was talking about, but in many meetings, my suggestions were ignored. Then, several minutes later, I would hear that same suggestion, which was deemed good by the group. This made me angry enough to not contribute anything else, which was wrong. Instead, I had to beat them at their prejudice game. I later learned that if I were presenting anything, I would go to each group member before the meeting and "run" my idea by them. I would get their feedback and then ask, "If I can incorporate these ideas into the solution, would you support it?" This approach seemed to work best for me.

Another challenge was to recognize the best leadership style for me. I had to be true to my authentic self. Consequently, the situational leadership style got me the results that I needed to be an impactful leader. So many of the male managers who used the command-and-control leadership style felt that the situational leadership style was a "weak" way to lead. But this style allowed me to meet the employees where they were, relative to their skill level, and help them to grow and feel good about their contributions to the team. Not only did I see the results, but year after year, my employee survey results were consistently high. Now, upper management was asking me why my ratings were so high. It was a little lesson that I learned from Sunday school: treat people the way that you want to be treated. It works!

JACKIE'S BEST ADVICE

- **Culture:** Find a culture that supports your style by allowing you to be your authentic self. This is the place where you will thrive.

- **Strengths:** Know your strengths and leverage them. What are the skills and competencies that you need to be an expert? You do not have to be an expert in everything. Identify, reach out, and leverage those resources where you are not strong.

- **Skills:** Build critical skills such as listening, decision making, problem solving, communications, presentation, critical thinking, business acumen, and technology. Stay current on the technology in your industry. These skills will help you grow your executive presence, be more strategic, and lead with a vision.

- **Relationships:** Build and leverage relationships. Seek out sponsors, mentors, and role models.

- **Saying "no" is an option:** Be sensitive to when it is okay to say "no" or that your plate is full. Taking on everything can quickly lead to burnout.

- **Asking for what you want:** If you do not ask, how will anyone know what you want (e.g., negotiate salary, promotion,)? So just do your homework first and be prepared with a plan B.

- **Being curious:** Curiosity will help you put the puzzle pieces together and open doors to new ideas and opportunities.

- **Politics:** Strategic relationships will help you to navigate through the political jungle just a little bit easier. Use those relationships. They are necessary.

- **Balance:** Integrating your work and personal life is a challenge, but it is a must! Delegate more. You do not have to do it all.

What is driving you to want to be a leader? To help you gain more clarity, take a few minutes to answer these questions.

1. Who are your mentors?

2. What qualities do you admire most about your mentors?

3. What can you do so that you are more like your mentors?

4. What is your personal brand? How does it set you apart?

5. What are your challenges and fears?

6. What stresses you to no end?

7. What brings you joy?

8. What mental shift is necessary to be an impactful leader?

9. When you look ahead ten or twenty years from now, where do you want to be? What do you want to accomplish? What do you want people to say about you?

Let me leave you with this excerpt from Marianne Williamson's *A Return to Love: Reflections on the Principles of A Course in Miracles*:

> Our deepest fear is not that we are inadequate. Our deepest fear is that we are powerful beyond measure. It is our light, not our darkness that most frightens us. Your playing small does not serve the world. We are all meant to shine.

ABOUT JACKIE

Jackie Stallings Evans is the President and CEO of What Do You Do When Leadership, Inc, a minority and woman-owned management consulting, leadership development, coaching, and training firm headquartered in Atlanta, Georgia. Jackie understands what it takes to be an impactful leader. She has worked as a corporate leader in the public, private, and government sectors for over thirty years. Her experience comes from having "walked in your shoes" as a leader. She knows what it is like to lead when the only thing constant is change. Having worked in corporate sales, learning and development, and government organizations, she has gained experience in management, consulting, coaching, training, sales, brand management, and business development. This combination of experiences allows her to work effectively with leaders at all levels and help them be more effective and impactful.

Jackie is certified as a Woman-Owned Small Business (WOSB); Women's Business Enterprise National Council (WBENC); a certified coach with the International Coaching Federation (ICF); a board-certified coach for the Center for Credentialing and Education (CCE); a Marshall Goldsmith Certified Stakeholder Centered Coach; and a certified Situational Leadership practitioner. She is certified to deliver the Myers-Briggs Type Indicator (MBTI), FIRO-B Assessment, the 360 Leadership Circle, and the Global Leadership 360 Assessment.

FILL YOUR TANK WITH THE POSITIVE

Paris Forest

IT Senior Director of End User Services,
The Boeing Company

PARIS'S PATH TO LEADERSHIP

I was thrown into corporate leadership kicking and screaming. I've
been a leader my entire life. No matter how much I may have tried
to blend in and just be a part of the crowd, I could never do it. One
way or another, I would wind up getting voted, asked, or assigned to
lead an activity to completion. This pattern started in middle school
and has continued to this day. In my formative years, my insecurities
would have made this a panic-inducing prospect, but later in life,
I have learned to embrace them. I have learned to regard it as an

honor to have natural attributes and qualities that cause others to push me forward when, in the past, fear would have me stand back.

I finally said "yes" to corporate leadership after turning down at least four leaders who asked me if I thought I might want to consider a shift in my career to a management track. I, like many, had had some bad experiences with mangers that really made me shy away from the possibility. I just didn't think that there was a place for a person with my mindset or leadership style. It was not until I decided there was no more running from the inevitable and accepted the right opportunity for me that my mindset shifted and I became focused on representing a different possibility for leadership in our environment. This intention and commitment to authenticity not only enabled a successful path to execute complicated and different styles of work, but it became a vehicle by which I could showcase the talent of others. Leaning more into my strengths as a talent manager, I was able to accelerate the value I delivered to our organization and expand my brand as a leader in the company.

The most interesting part of how I came to be in the leadership role that I hold now is that it is directly attributed to a video project in a leadership class. The class was to help high-potential leaders in the area of functional excellence, and the champion for the week was a VP with whom I hadn't had much opportunity to work. He'd heard of me but had no clue what I could do. Our team decided to do our program report as a video because one of our teammates had to leave early. Actually, I had recommended we do that so that everyone could be involved. The video and the leadership impressed this VP so much that he took our report and showed it at the next CIO staff meeting. This changed the entire trajectory of my career and is the moment that I credit with creating the kind of career capital needed to spark the development discussions that elevate employees in large firms like mine.

PARIS'S GREATEST CHALLENGE

My greatest challenge as a leader was getting the chip off of my shoulder. I know that may sound odd to some, but the reality is that most of the challenges that I faced as a leader were as a result of mismanagement of relationships. I've always been strong and strong-willed and willing to step to the front of any line. That wasn't always celebrated coming from a woman, and it was absolutely criticized coming from a woman of color. Over time, and unbeknownst to me, the chip on my shoulder went from a small sliver to a boulder. I believe that what we carry in our lives, we convey. I had a heavy burden from years of sediment that I allowed to build up as a result of the behavior of others.

I recently had the opportunity for myself and a group of others to attend an eight-week leadership course at a nationally branded professional development company. It was during a reflection exercise, when we were setting goals for our outcomes, that I had a startling epiphany: I was good at recovering but not at creating relationships. My goal was to never have a person I had to partner with say to me, "I love working with you now, but I hated you when I met you." Up to that point in my career, I'd heard that exact sentence more than once. I'd always chalked it up to the other person, but what I had to own was that the problem started with me. I was a hurt person who showed up hurt no matter how hard I tried to hide it. It didn't matter if I had a magical smile or a quick wit or if I would do anything to see another person succeed; their experience of me in part or in total left them feeling the weight of my burdens.

I had to address it, but first I had to own it. I had to sit in the reality that many of my relationship challenges could easily be blamed on any number of the applicable *isms* (and some were absolutely compounded by the *isms*), but the root started with me. I came to the table with unconfirmed biases around the intents of others and allowed those biases to drive my responses to behavior that confirmed the boulder on my shoulder. After owning that I had been party to some of my own displeasure, I took steps to seek feedback from others. I was already in a professional development program, so I took it seriously. I worked that program, and I was intentional about creating immediate opportunities to practice what I had learned. I found out that there were more people who wanted to help me than wanted to harm me. I owned my part of the problem, I sought out a potential solution, and then, when I knew better, I *did* better. I'm happy to report that I've now had the opportunity to lead three teams since this work, and not once has anyone loved me after hating me.

PARIS'S BEST ADVICE

The best advice that I would give a woman with her eye on leadership is to learn to willingly accept positive feedback and encouragement. There is a power that is created when we are willing to believe a thing. What I have found through my journey to leadership is that I was not able to achieve the audacious goals that I had in the secret places of my heart and my mind until I was willing to accept positivity from others regarding my capabilities and my potential. I can literally go back in my mind and remember the number of times that I've received comments such as "We'll all be working for you one day" or "You're going to be the next [insert high-ranking executive position]." Until about three years ago, I would always respond with self-deprecation or deflection. Internally, it was as if I would not be able to achieve those things if I didn't respond to the recognition with a certain level of humility. As I started to get feedback on my leadership journey that I was much more critical of myself than others were, I wanted to understand more. So, I took the next available opportunity to dig in and assess what was causing me to see myself in such a negative light.

During my time studying for my Executive MBA, I recognized that my reflex was to absorb constructive—and even negative—feedback and deflect the positive. I had spent most of my youth perceiving myself as an underdog, so negative energy was my fuel. If I was told I couldn't do something, not only was I going to do it, but I was going to do it so well that you could never challenge me again. This worked well until it didn't. The unintended consequence was that I couldn't perform if I didn't think that someone was challenging my capability. It was as if seeing myself as capable and full of potential for great things would make me weak instead of strong. While I was able to hone a large skill set and achieve some great things, I was editing myself out of my own story. I learned through a lot more error than trial that I needed to accept that positive reinforcement because it was confirming what was coded inside of me.

I know you have experienced it: you hear the same piece of positive feedback from totally unrelated people. You deflect the affirmation because affirmation feels funny, and then you note that this person is the umpteenth person to say the exact same thing. The messaging isn't wrong; the mailbox isn't working. To quote my pastor, "What you feed grows, and what you starve dies." Allow the deliveries and deposits you keep to be those that confirm the positive things about you. The other items are just data points to consider and delete upon evaluation; the positivity is seeds that need to be planted in you so that your destiny can bloom. My best advice is to fill your tank with the positive and eliminate the negative.

ABOUT PARIS

Paris Forest is the IT Sr. Director of End User Services at The Boeing Company, responsible for defining, delivering, and continually improving workplace productivity and collaboration capabilities to drive impeccable user experience, generate business value, and cultivate efficiencies for the Boeing Enterprise, including col-  laboration services, desktop and mobility technology, unified communications services, and print management services.

Paris joined The Boeing Company in May of 1999, after two internships, and has held various technical and leadership positions in the Boeing Information Technology & Data Analytics (IT&DA) organization. During her time with the company, Paris has been instrumental in leading key efforts and cross-functional business and technology teams on major capital and noncapital programs and projects. Prior to her current position, Paris was the Director of Strategy Operations Solutions, responsible for defining strategy and action planning for initiatives aimed at transforming IT&DA from a project-driven to product-managed organization at scale. In this role, Paris served as the Optimal Enterprise Integration Program Director, responsible for executing the technology integration of seventeen subsidiary businesses into the Boeing Enterprise, focused on reduction of risk and increase of technology value. Paris also served at the Technology Business Management (TBM)

Office Director, responsible for implementing and operationalizing IT&DA's Technology Business Management solution. Paris is the proud parent of one phenomenal twelve-year-old and spends her free time enjoying his schooling and sporting activities, traveling, reading, going to movies, and participating in church and community events.

Paris holds her Bachelor of Science in Biology from Missouri Baptist University and Executive MBA from Washington University Olin Business School. Paris was most recently recognized by the St. Louis Business Journal as a part of the 2020 Class of Most Influential Women in Business, an award that spotlights the women making the biggest impact at their company and in the community. In 2019, she was awarded The St. Louis American Newspaper's 2019 Salute to Business—Excellence in Business Performance Award. Nationally, Paris was one of the 2018 Women of Color in Technology, receiving the New Media/IT Leadership Award; at Boeing, she was awarded the 2018 St. Louis Site Diversity and Inclusion Executive Walk the Talk Award, given to one executive at the St. Louis site who is recognized for "an achievement of distinction for doing the right thing, leading by example and making it happen."

In the community, Paris serves on the Board of Trustees for the St. Louis Science Center and the Board of Directors for Webster Child Care Center, a quality provider of care and education for children six weeks to six years of age with a focus on social-emotional and academic preparedness and scholarship programs for families in crisis. Paris also represents The Boeing Company on the Champions Board of the National Girls Collaborative Project, a national project connecting organizations working to advance the agenda in gender equity and encouraging girls to pursue careers in STEM.

Paris is also a champion for the Ora Lee Smith Cancer Research Foundation, working to reach a fundraising goal of $10 million to start human trials on an advanced laser/nanoparticle therapy proven to destroy tumors in mice, in fifteen days, with no observable side effects.

YOU BECOME WHAT YOU THINK ABOUT ALL DAY

Tina Frey Clements
Vice President

TINA'S PATH TO LEADERSHIP

Right place, right time, right attitude. I have always been in the "people business," working in learning and development, talent management, training, HR, etc. This path did not begin with a plan, however. At the start of my career, I was more of a grasshopper than an ant, enjoying what I was doing and not really planning for the future. When I started in the automotive industry and facilitated with regularity, that's when I fell in love. There's nothing more amazing than seeing an "ah-ha" moment first-hand. I love witnessing a person learning something new, accepting something about him/herself or shifting his/her perspective. It's spectacular. And as a result, the groundwork for my path was laid. As I grew as a facilitator, I also grew as a leader and sought out feedback from those I admired. New opportunities to grow while leading presented themselves until, ultimately, I was offered the chance to create an entire company that delivers "ah-ha" moments to others. I feel strongly that I subconsciously created my path and was actively open to growth opportunities along the way. I'm living proof that you become what you think about all day long.

TINA'S GREATEST CHALLENGE

When BMW asked me to launch their new joint venture called The Retail Performance in the United States, the "noise" in my head told me I was too stupid to be successful. And for a long time, I listened. I was held hostage by the "noise" telling me I wasn't good enough. When I accepted the fact that this "noise" was there to keep me safe and to keep me from failing, I was able to thank the "noise" for caring, but also tell it, "I've got this." Shifting my perspective to appreciate the "noise" and then changing the script was so very hard. However, as a result, I approach all current roadblocks with awareness, ownership, and action. Thanks. "noise," but again, "I've got this."

TINA'S BEST ADVICE

Make good choices. The world can be hard: unforgiving, unflattering, and sometimes all-around not nice. It's the same world for everyone; however, how you choose to approach it is up to you. Will you react or respond? Will you choose to shift your perspective around a situation or become a victim to your circumstances?

It's your choice. The moment you find yourself in the blame game is actually the moment the game is over—and you lost. Decide how you want to show up, then show up. Know that nothing is happening "to you"; is just happening. The best advice I can give is that when you hit that roadblock—and you certainly will—accept it, own it, shift your perspective around it, and then get busy changing it. You've got this.

ABOUT TINA

Tina Frey Clements is a high-energy Keynote Speaker, Author, Facilitator, Coach, and successful executive. Before being asked to launch the BMW Group Joint Venture, The Retail Performance Company, LLC (rpc) in 2013, she was a prominent leader in the BMW Organization and has been in the learning and development industry since 1996.

Within BMW, her responsibilities included actively leading the company's performance management, professional development, and training. Tina's vast experiences have helped define and create the rpc brand and are helping to elevate and develop the future talent of rpc, the BMW Group, and other organizations.

Prior to BMW, Tina led initiatives and grew talent within organizations such as HBO, Volkswagen, IBM, and WVIP. She has held leadership positions such as vice president, operations director, and training manager throughout her career and excels at moving businesses forward and motivating and growing talent.

Tina not only talks the talk; she walks the walk. Always challenging herself to improve and grow, she has earned her CPC and ELI-MP accreditations, among others, including DiSC®, MBTI®, and Langevin.

Tina believes a company's success is directly related to the overall engagement of its people. She has dedicated her career to sharing ideas, methods, and messages to help leaders elevate up and over their personal roadblocks to find success and focus on what's important. Leaders are not responsible to make people happy. They are, however, responsible for creating an environment of trust, where people thrive, feel empowered, and can't wait to make good choices. This is how you create engagement. This is how you create loyalty. And ultimately, this is how you grow your business.

PART THREE

IT'S OKAY TO BE PROVOCATIVE

Desireè Hardge
CEO and Founder, Convenire International

"To live is to challenge yourself, to go beyond what you cannot see, to run the distances without looking back, and to rely on your faith to see you through." – Desireè Hardge

DESIREÈ'S PATH TO LEADERSHIP

It chose me; I did not choose it. I know it sounds cliché; however, from an early age I had a feeling that I had a gift and it started to foster in my formative years in elementary school when my classmates would stop and listen to what I had to say or follow my directions. Regardless if they were misunderstandings—it was about doing the right thing, "do good be good." Like the time in fourth grade when I was managing a snack bar and gave away most of the food because some students did not have money to buy anything and they were hungry. What was I supposed to do? Let them starve? My intentions were good; however, the Vice Principal did not see it that way and gave me detention. I think the late Congressman John Lewis would call that "good trouble."

During those formative years, I had a sense that I could command the attention from others by my spoken words, as I had always been a thoughtful thinker and my peers often followed my lead as a genuine and inclusive person. For years, I did not fully understand my natural abilities to lead others, even when I played sports in high school or volunteered. I began stepping into leadership roles during and after college, becoming a lead Legal Assistant at a prominent law firm; then transitioning to holding the position of Research, Data, and Evaluation Manager in Early Childhood Development and Community; and finally, owning a Business Consulting firm and becoming Vice President of Development for a breast cancer nonprofit. Through those positions, my platform expanded with professionals from various industries and background that called upon me for my experience, knowledge, and "get s*** done" demeanor. From this, I understand business totality; what it means to have authentic and meaningful relationships; and more importantly, my values, ethics, morals and worldly vision of who I am as a thought leader.

Throughout the years, I have come to understand that a person is born a natural leader, is trained to be a leader, pretends to be a leader because it "looks good," or is pressured to be a leader for face value. These variables of leadership can inevitably affect a person's success and misguide those they lead, but ultimately it is the leader's belief, faith, and perseverance coupled with one's authentic self that allow you to be successful.

My leadership journey has been shaped by many people and elements through aspiring to educate myself on various subject matters, living and working in diverse communities, and unapologetically empowering people to be their best selves. I realized that if I could impact someone's life positively, then many others would be impacted by that person. That is called "reciprocity."

Throughout my professional career, I have met interesting people from all walks of life. And in one form or another I have learned something from them about myself or the complexity of humanity. Some I still call my friends or acquaintances I run into at networking events, and then there are those I would rather forget about—but without burning bridges, as one never knows if a person or organization will come back in a different professional form.

> "It is the mark of an educated mind to entertain a thought without accepting it." – Aristotle

Just like the eclectic music I listen to... the people I call my friends are no different. My friends range from C-suite leaders that oversee Fortune 500 companies and gun-toting cowboys that generously donate to inner-city youth because he believes that every child should have a chance at a quality life to an eco-friendly anti-fracking feminists that teach children yoga in school classrooms and janitors at my local grocery store and everyone in between. These are people I am honored and grateful to call my friends as they have hearts of gold with impeccable leadership skills and integrity that beckons me to be an efficacious leader.

"Treat everyone as if they are an executive because you never know if they are or will be one day. Plus it's the right thing to do." – Desireè Hardge

I have witnessed for the past thirty-seven years that genuine people possess an ability to speak life into those they meet and positively transform things that they touch. I have a profound belief that everyone has a purpose and deserves to achieve their greatest potential on this journey called life and to not be denied nor suppressed on the bases of race, religion, gender, socioeconomic status, or geographic location.

It would be erroneous of me to not speak on the challenges that I have come up against along the way. I have been in uncomfortable positions before. The ones that make you question, am I good enough or do I belong here at this meeting with high level executives. Or when I was being bullied and threatened by a former employer. My intellect, talent, and morals were being suppressed, stolen, and tested; as I was maligned while working in an hostile environment and being able to do my job effectively and efficiently became a fight. It was a position that I loved, held respect for, and great work was being done for communities in underserved areas. Arising from that obstacle I learned that, even in tribulation, God is my greatest strength and encouragement. The lesson I learned from that chapter, never dim my light [star] for those that choose not to see me. Instead I continue to walk with grace as my purpose and dignity.

For years, I worked under those who failed to see my value and those that stole my ideas. I realized creating my own space would be the best way to set sail on the vast sea called prosperity and purpose. Truth be told, no one was going to do it for me, and it was time for me to do—forge ahead and blaze my own trail—something I had felt my whole life. I realized I had to stop building organizations for others and start building my own legacy—not to be an icon but to create an idea. In doing so, I took back the power of being viewed as expendable as if I was a character in the movie *The Expendables*, starring Sylvester Stallone. It is an action thriller featuring a group of former elite soldiers who fought for their country, only to be abandoned and hunted by the same organization that employed them a decade before. I have optimistically concluded that I would rather own and sail my own boat and choose my destination than to have it hijacked.

It would be remiss if I did not speak briefly on "imposter syndrome," which is the feeling of not being good enough to lead or be in the same space (voice at a table) with influential leaders, even though God has shown that you belong there just as much as those who are already there. Like most people, I have had to deal with this. I needed to believe in myself and get out of my own way, regard-less of what people thought of me. I also understood it's okay to be provocative, and ruffling some feathers along the way, and to push myself beyond my comfort-zone. Being provocative is to stimulate your mindset to think outside the box, not in the context of sex-ual arousal, rather positive empowerment and reinforcement from within to reach your goals and the desires of your heart in life. To become unstoppable and unapologetic for aspiring to be more than just...

My list of individuals that I consider some of the greatest lead-ers in history include the Greek philosopher Socrates, who laid the groundwork for Western logic and philosophy; Maya Angelou, who wrote several trail-blazing books and spoke prophetically on the subject of civil rights and an advocate for humanity; Nelson

Mandela, who helped to end apartheid in South Africa and became its president; Cesar Chavez, who was a civil rights activist and labor leader, and Oprah Winfrey, who became the first African-American and woman billionaire. All struggled with doubt, trauma, uncertainty, and adversity, but through it all, they knew they were leaders and had a purpose. And regardless of where they came from, with the many hurdles they overcame they had something to share with the world that was bigger than themselves.

After getting past self-doubt and with a fire still abundantly burning inside of me to thrive, I decided to jump in and lean forward and founded Convenire International. As founder and CEO, I decide that my organizational mission would be to identify, pursue, and develop strategic opportunities through business development and fundraising to cultivate partnerships in the non-for-profit and for-profit sectors. We pride ourselves on being able to foster creative solutions while building long-term market value for our clients and global communities.

DESIREÈ'S GREATEST CHALLENGE

Going back to "imposter syndrome"—the feeling of being inadequate to what current culture deems as valuable or worthy—as confident as I have been most of my life, there have been times when I have felt like throwing in the towel because it would be easier than to weather the storms that felt like an endless tsunami. But there was always a voice perched on my shoulder—a gut feeling—that told me to never give up, coupled with the power of positive thinking that has often attracted positive energy and quality people into my life. Most importantly, as a spiritual person, I have always had God at the core of all that I am and what I do, like the guiding light of a lighthouse.

In the movie *Wonder Woman*, the title character is traveling with the British Army, that is going from town to town and liberating communities, when they come under hostile fire. Wonder Woman decides to step out of the bunker to charge forward regardless. She finds herself alone in the middle of a field as her male counterparts are hunkered down in the bunker. As she gets closer to the opposition, she realizes she needs to protect herself better as the fire power proves to be too strong. Wonder Woman puts her shield in front to protect herself. Eventually, she makes her way forward and liberates another town.

That scene brought me to tears, as I could relate to Wonder Woman, metaphorically. As a woman and a woman of color, I take on many transgressions from those that have tried to devalue me as a person, and I feel the ongoing rapid fire that comes with being a thought leader. Through it all, like Wonder Women, I continue to engage in the battle, knowing there is something bigger than I can see and what others know and speak. I choose to continue to move uphill, knowing that there will be battles along the way and self-doubt, like the 6th Marine Division faced when it took the hill called Sugar Loaf during World War II. My hill is to claim a slice of the "American Dream."

It would be erroneous of me to think, as I move forward as a leader, that there will be no opposition. Unfortunately, that comes with the landscape no matter how positive and optimistic I remain. However because I know who I am, I know who I am *not*. If I stay true to myself and keep my morals, ethics, and integrity intact, then those who come against me shall fail and only strengthen the person I become tomorrow.

> "Let us throw off everything that hinders and the sin that so easily entangles. And let us run with perseverance the race marked out for us. Fixing our eyes on Jesus." – Hebrews 12:1

DESIREÈ'S BEST ADVICE

The advice I would give women is to never give in or give up and to remain unapologetically positive even when you can't see a way, your God has a way. To sharpen and equip your mind with a vast understanding of business, industries, and people from all walks of life. Your mind is the most powerful tool in your arsenal that you will forever nourish and carry: guard it like Fort Knox.

Never stop learning and growing in your personal and professional life, make helping others your aphrodisiac, and know your worth and value. Remove yourself from those individuals or groups that do not see the amazing woman you are, who do not feed your soul with fruitfulness, and who hold you back from becoming the incredible woman that you know you can be. Respect those who have come before you that offer guidance and wisdom. Take it all in like a sponge dipped in water, soak up what you need and dispose of the rest. Always apply the Golden Rule, treat others the way you want to be seen and treated.

Know that it is okay to be provocative and to say "no." Eyes may roll, and tables may be flipped (figuratively); but any great leader—especially businesswomen whether you're in finance, medicine, business, technology, politics, law, accounting, real estate, etc.—knows that you cannot please everyone (that is exhausting) nor should you try, and stand your ground.

To be a successful, thoughtful, and effective leader, you must be willing to be the face of change, have a voice of wisdom, be uncomfortable, and drown out the negative critics. As former First Lady Michelle Obama once said, "When they go low, we go high."

If I received a dollar for every person, including friends and family, who spoke ill about me, told me I would never amount to anything, looked down upon me, or dismissed me; I could have made it a part-time job. Remember, people are only human. They do not know your destiny, and you yourself may not see it right now nor feel it. But I promised you, if you keep swimming like Dory in *Nemo*—"just keep swimming, just keep swimming"—you will not only overcome whatever fears or insecurities you feel confined by, you will begin to truly live your purpose, thrive, and become a better, healthier, and brilliantly you.

My track coach used to tell me, "Desireè, imagine yourself placing first and crossing the finish line." And I did. He would say, "Do not worry about those around you to your left or right, or look back to see how close others are because you will lose speed and diminish your focus." For years that advice has stayed with me, and I have applied it in my daily life and as a leader. I share it with you. There will always be someone better than you, who is smarter, younger, faster, prettier, more educated, etc. It is inevitable. When you remain steadfast or come into focus, like binoculars that have just been adjusted, your vision and mission are illuminated, your problems begin to dissolve, and those who are your competitors seem to become obsolete or invisible as you excel. That is not to say, do not stop and smell the roses and take a victory lap for all that you have accomplished or will achieve. You can only be as great as your mind, body, and spirit allow and from the amount of personal investment you put in yourself.

The fact that you are reading this book puts you a step closer to becoming the leader you have always felt yourself to be. Never give up! I am rooting for you and the many women who are ready to write a new chapter and live their best life. Salud!

ABOUT DESIREÈ

Desireè Hardge, is the Founder, Chief Executive Officer of Convenire International. She is an Arizonan and has over eighteen years of combined experience in the for-profit and nonprofit sectors. As a former Vice President of Development for a prominent nonprofit, she continues to acquire new skill sets and business relations that make her an effective business leader and an expert in her field. She strategically leads organizations through business development to help acquire capital, maintain and improve client retention, fundraise and event manage, build market and brand significance, and improve consumer loyalty.

Desireè is a mother to four beautiful daughters. As a single working mom, she put herself through undergraduate and graduate school. She holds an MBA from the University of Phoenix and has numerous certificates, including Executive Leadership from Social Venture Partners (SVP-AZ). She is a business board advisor, member of Phoenix Committee on Foreign Relations (PCFR), and an alumna of Collaborative 2019. Most importantly a child of God.

In her spare time, she loves being outdoors, paddle boarding, running, attending art galleries, going to festivals and listening to live music, wine vineyards, practicing hot yoga, and taking in theatre.

LOOK BEYOND THE TITLE TO SEE THE BIG PICTURE

Vicki Wright-Hamilton
Change Management Strategist

VICKI'S PATH TO LEADERSHIP

My work experience in high school and college set me on a trajectory of managing people incredibly early on in my career. My first leadership position started just nine months after I began my career. I was given the opportunity to utilize my technology skills and previous work experience to develop a brand-new operations department. I was ecstatic that I had a chance to use my knowledge for a greater purpose. It was at this time that I found out the importance of paying your dues and believing in yourself and your abilities to change the status quo.

I became known as an expert in my field, which centered around IBM AS/400s. I quickly earned a reputation for operational excellence. During that time, I was known as a key person to develop operations policy and procedures. I was also well versed in helping both our clients and technology teams understand their roles in executing business strategy.

I built my career by taking on projects that others did not want to do or perceived as being too risky. I was willing to take on the risky projects to learn something new and add new tools to my toolbox, so that I could prepare for future opportunities.

After decades as a senior executive, I was laid off during the 2008 recession. I then found myself thrust into a different leadership capacity, as the CEO and Founder of my very own firm, VWH Consulting. For a decade, I served as a visionary leader for my own organizational strategy and mission. It has been a lot of hard work. While I ultimately choose whom I would like to work with, the fact remains that I must still show up as a leader for my staff and clients. I must still earn the trust of each client and team member who works alongside me, which is ultimately what it means to be a leader. For me, being a leader is motivating people to work towards a common goal. I do this by building authentic relationships with my clients and employees.

VICKI'S GREATEST CHALLENGE

My greatest challenge as a leader has been being a Black female executive. I have always been perceived as the token black in the technology industry, which is dominated by white men. We all know that diversity and inclusion (D&I) have been buzzwords in recent years. In my career, the need for D&I ranged from the need to meet affirmative-action quotas to the desire of wanting to get more Black women into leadership in technology. I made a vow to myself that I would help other minorities get exposed to the opportunities that were available in technology.

When you find yourself as the only person of color, specifically the only Black person, you are under a microscope. In those days, and still today, you constantly must prove that you have earned your seat at that table. There are colleagues and clients who make assumptions about who you are and how you got to where you are, without having any idea of the impact that you are having on the bottom line of the business. Some people are verbal and will outright question your validity of being in that professional space, while others are quietly observing your behavior and your career journey.

I was considered by quite a few peers and other leaders to be that exception. My question was "An exception to what?" What in the world does that mean? It was explained to me that because I could speak well and dressed nicely and knew my stuff, I was not like other minorities. I must admit that I was shocked that these kinds of comments would be spoken aloud. Even more terrifying is that the executives in several organizations for which I have worked genuinely believed this was the case. I began to ask for further clarification regarding the intent of the comments. I was told that I fit the model of someone they would like to represent the company in public. My command of words, my presentation, my dress, and my looks were aligned. I wanted to know more. I was not as wise as I am today, and I really struggled. I have to admit a lot of my struggles also came from other Black people telling me that I got to where I was only because of how I looked: a black woman with light skin and long black hair. I was the closest to looking and speaking like my white counterparts. Now, I can write a book on the challenges within my own community. At the end of the day, I was able to help other Black people of every shade advance their careers.

I understood that I could create a path for other minorities only by earning my seat at the table. I earned that seat by helping various departments and organizations increase their bottom line. I put myself out there to start diversity councils and get involved with the company challenges. I wanted to be part of the solution, to make a difference, and I promoted other diverse candidates. I always had an open door to everyone (cleaners, security guards, cafeteria workers, assistants, employees, other leaders). I have always been committed to exhibiting behaviors that showed I was truly a cause-driven leader. In the end, I became a well-respected senior executive who not only had a seat at the table with a voice but one who has been heard and heeded. I am not just a pretty black face to be served a plate of food and told to be quiet.

VICKI'S BEST ADVICE

As women, we believe we must be like a man in the office to succeed. We need to do things their way, and we cannot really be ourselves. I completely understand this thought process; however, I think we can learn from them and still be ourselves. Your authenticity is what makes you unique and allows for you to think outside of the box. When we are not authentic, we add a lot of stress to our lives. We are trying to be someone else and act the way that they want us to versus showing our perspective, sharing ideas, and solving problems in a different way. It is also important to know and understand the boundaries of the culture in which you are operating. If the culture limits you from being your true self and does not allow for a diversity of thought, then you may need to consider if it is the right place for you.

Each of us has a power of influence. Your ability to influence others is critical as you move forward. You gain that power through communication, seeking to understand before being understood and seeking respect for yourself as a person, for your functional knowledge, and for your ability to get others to want to follow you. If you are a leader of others, and they are not willing to follow you, they are just complying. This is when you should do some introspection to ensure you are doing everything you can to show up as a true leader. This respect goes beyond your company, to other companies within your industry and functional expertise.

Throughout one's career, you may have to make choices on your direction. Those choices can range from taking a step backwards or sideways, or taking another position that keeps you at the same level. You should always look at any move as an opportunity to learn and grow, regardless of the level. We can sometimes get so hooked on titles that we miss the big picture of making the impact we are striving to accomplish. I encourage you to look at the pros and cons of any opportunity and really think about the benefits and potential learning. This is what I refer to as taking calculated risks when you understand how you will use the opportunity to move forward down the road. This gives you the ability to make an impact.

As a leader, it is critical to get involved with industry associations from both a company and a functional perspective. There is power in others knowing you as a person and your capabilities, and in having exposure. As you participate in these organizations and get your personal brand on the radar, your company begins to take notice. They begin to understand your external power of influence, as well as how much others respect your knowledge. This is the spot that you want to be in, as you never know when one of these relationships can play an important role in your next opportunity. It is also important to note that they may be your sponsor at the table, speaking on your behalf without your knowledge. So, always get involved and do not just bury yourself at work or sit in your office. That does not serve you well!

I am a firm believer that everyone needs to understand one's own value. As you move within your career, your value should increase with your knowledge and skills. You can do this by staying on top of job openings of interest. At least once a year, you should apply and follow through with an interview. This allows you to see what is available, what is happening at other companies, and what skills and experience are worth. There is nothing like getting another offer and having the power of choice—to move on to another organization if you decide. You will never know if you do not seek to find out.

ABOUT VICKI

An accomplished technology leader with over twenty years of experience in highly matrixed organizations, Vicki Wright-Hamilton is a change management expert, corporate strategist/coach, and best-selling author.

Vicki currently serves as president and CEO of VWH Consulting, a firm she developed to help companies flex and align their strategic approaches with the fast-paced, ever-changing technological business environments in order to remain relevant and competitive. As a consultant to some of the world's most recognizable brands, Vicki partners with executive game changers to develop and execute a broad range of organizational and revenue improvements.

Vicki's first book, *Game Face: Corporate Success Strategies of a Trailblazing Tech Warrior,* invites readers to take a powerful journey with her—a self-driven force of nature, passionate female, and proud African-American, who happens to also be a tech-savvy phenom. She offers an intimate look at the challenges of technology from a woman's perspective and, through personal and professional accounts, shares unprecedented takeaways to help organizations successfully recruit and retain diverse talent while avoiding the common pitfalls destined to cripple companies that, for whatever reason, do not seek and embrace the technological prowess and contributions of female women of color.

Vicki is the former president of Women in Technology (WIT) and currently serves on the organization's advisory board. She also serves on the Board of Growing Leaders, a dynamic leadership program that prepares tomorrow's leaders for succession opportunities.

In 2017, Vicki became a Board Member for the Technical Association of Georgia (TAG). She was a member of the Women in Technology Foundation Board from 2005 until 2018 and them became a member of the Women in Technology (WIT) Advisory Board from 2018 until the time of this writing. Vicki was also a Global Executive with the Women Board Breakthrough Leadership division at Time Warner and attended the Betsy Magness Leadership

Institute. She has completed the Landmark Communications Executive Leadership Program and completed the Leadership and Development-Effective Leadership Program at the Center for Creative. Vicki is an Executive Board Member with the National Urban League's Black Executive Exchange Program (BEEP), former president of the National Association for Multi-ethnicity in Communications-Atlanta, and she is the former IT Director for the National Black MBA-Atlanta.

Vicki is the proud mother of two adult sons, Arthur—who's married to Angelica—and Brandon, and is an over-the-moon grandmother to one. She and her husband, Harold, reside in Atlanta, Georgia.

THE RELUCTANT LEADER

Kiala Givehand
LifeAlchemist™ and Happiness Catalyst

KIALA'S PATH TO LEADERSHIP

It didn't always feel like it, but looking back now, I realize that I've always been a leader. In high school, I participated in several clubs (in and out of school), and I somehow always ended up in a leadership position in all of them. From achieving second chair in the band to an appointment as the manager of the dance team (that was probably because I was much better at managing than dancing), I had my fair share of leadership experiences before the age of eighteen. I might be what some people call a born leader, but that's looking in from the outside.

Internally, I've always felt happier, more confident, and better suited for working behind the scenes. One of my favorite jobs is that of a runner. I like being the one that runs to get other people coffee, to grab an extra binder for the conference presenter, or to pass out all the pens and supplies during a class. I do those things really well. And that's how it usually happened. I would do a great job, and those in charge took notice. That has been my path to leadership: being good at my job, no matter how small it seemed.

It's not that I'm better than the next person; it's that I take a little more pride in my work than most. Maybe it's the Capricorn in me (I like a good mountain to climb and a goal to reach), but I find it purposeful to do a thing and do it well. Maybe that is one of the hallmarks of a good leader.

From high school to college, not much changed. I became the kind of student who received average grades, was organized, and not afraid to speak up in class, and I worked quickly. These traits always got me noticed. During group assignments, I ultimately led my team, sometimes because no one else wanted the job and sometimes because I was absolutely the best person for the job (even though I was reluctant).

During the interview for my first post-college teaching job, the principal looked at my future department chair and said, "I know this will be her first year teaching, but let's send her to the summer workshop. She's going to be one of our school leaders." And I was. I became the technology liaison for the teachers, pioneered the first "computers in the classroom" initiative, trained 100+ seasoned writing teachers on how to support students as they learned to write more creatively, co-chaired the school's first Black History assembly, and was nominated to win Teacher of the Year in my first year of teaching. (I didn't win, but I did get awarded FIRST YEAR teacher of the year at my school.)

And that would be the defining trait of my 20+ year teaching career. I was often "voluntold" by my supervisors to lead this or that, nominated by my peers to represent them in one way or another, or selected by decision makers to be the one in charge.

It's interesting to look back at the series of events that have led to my ability to lead, and lead well. I saw every situation as a learning opportunity. Along the journey, I had excellent mentors and administrators, who not only saw a leader in me, but helped me cultivate that part of myself. In most instances, they selected me and guided me along the way. And with each role, I became more astute and adept at being a leader. I learned from my mistakes, and I genuinely wanted to do my best. I would compete with myself to be better in the next position than I had been in the previous one. And that is how my path kept evolving and how I became the kind of leader I am today.

KIALA'S GREATEST CHALLENGE

By far my greatest challenge has been overcoming age differences. Because I had years in leadership as a teenager, I stepped into adulthood with the skills of someone twenty years my senior. By the time I transitioned out of the classroom and into a teacher-trainer position, I had the confidence of a veteran teacher, but I was only twenty-four. The challenge of being a twenty-four-year-old teacher trainer is that I was training teachers who were old enough to be my mother, grandmother, even great grandmother. And some of them made sure I knew that right from the start.

The way I overcame that challenge was by being twice as prepared as most people. I remember one woman during my very first training who literally heckled me from the audience. It threw me off at first, but eventually I won her over. I knew my stuff, to put it mildly. I felt confident with the content, and I shared tried-and-true methods that worked in my classroom. When she realized I wasn't just reading from theoretical textbooks, she sang my praises. And this kind of challenge became the one thing that I found myself faced with until I hit my forties. There was always someone who required me to prove my ability, my worthiness, or my intelligence. It didn't stop me. Having to do that time and time again made me a stronger leader and actually fueled my preparedness and competency over the years.

KIALA'S BEST ADVICE

I've gathered, and held close on my path to leadership, the following four pieces of advice. They don't come from one source, but from a myriad of women who have mentored me (knowingly and unknowingly). These nuggets of wisdom now serve as my personal reminders.

1. Start from a place of love. As leaders, if we can remember that everything begins and ends with our love for one another, then we will have a much more pleasant experience on the road to becoming a leader. Release any unhealthy connections to the word "love." Get clear on your definition of the word at its purest level. Find resources that help you cultivate a culture of love with the people you are charged with leading. And surrender to the notion that leaders are only as good as those who follow them. Create loving followers so that they eventually become loving leaders.

2. Women in leadership have two very important gifts: the ability to nurture and the power to anticipate the needs of others. Master these gifts. Use them for good and lead with them as your compass pointing true north.

3. Intention and attention are tethered together in a way that makes them powerful allies on your road to leadership. Always set an intention when you're in a role of leadership. Set intentions at the start of your meeting, during your conversations with superiors, and when you question your ability to lead. Attention is the evidence that you are intentional and deliberate in your leadership. As James Redfield notes, where Attention goes Energy flows. Energy flows where attention goes.

4. Great leaders know how to be led. Put yourself in situations where you get to see others lead. This is how you learn where you are doing well and where you need more development. Watch how other leaders navigate conversations, how they handle obstacles and challenges, and how they motivate people to follow them. The best teacher is experience, and experience comes from sitting on both sides of the table, especially when it comes to leadership.

ABOUT KIALA

Kiala Givehand is a LifeAlchemist™ and Happiness Catalyst who guides women to and through creative and spiritual awakenings. She combines creativity with intuition, ancient guidance systems, and intentional self-study as a way to radically

cultivate happiness. Her deepest desire is to help women step into their greatness by helping them uncover (and write, draw, or paint) their unique story. Through her online programs, workshops, and master classes, Kiala provides a safe space for women to explore and discover their dreams. She is a Dreamweaver, a fountain pen collector, a SoulCollage® Facilitator, an Intuitive Guide, a bookbinder, and the creator of inspirational presentations, books, and retreats. You can connect more fully with Kiala in one of her online classes or on Instagram (@kialagives).

TAKE A SEAT AT THE TABLE AND FOCUS ON HIGH-PROFILE TASKS

Kate Fitzgerald
Sales Leader

KATE'S PATH TO LEADERSHIP

A chance put me on my path to leadership. My first manager, Janet, took a chance hiring me into my first professional job with no experience but a huge drive to succeed. Fifteen years and hundreds of interviews later, as both the interviewer and interviewee, I still remember my interview with Janet and the terrifying excitement of what this interview could mean for my future. As in almost every interview since, Janet asked me to give her an example of a time when I overcame an obstacle. Throughout college, I had worked at the mall and somehow managed to connect my experience selling blue jeans to high school- and college-age women to managing a million-dollar outside sales territory. I wasn't close to having 100% of the job's required qualifications, but Janet saw something in me and took a chance.

Initially, it was the chance that Janet took to hire me with no previous experience, but what really allowed me to earn a leadership role in only five years was Janet's mentorship. At the start of our work together, Janet was just a good manager, developing my skills and instilling confidence in me. This great management coupled with my drive to succeed meant I had a successful tenure as sales representative.

The Association for Talent Development says, "A good mentor can help the mentee become more effective at work, learn new skills, develop greater confidence, and make better decisions for their overall career growth." This is exactly how Janet supported me.

Janet ensured I didn't just do good work, but that important people knew about my good work. It was her mentorship that ensured my skills and accomplishments stood out to our company's distributed executive team. She helped me make connections throughout the organization. Her introductions to the company's leadership provided me with opportunities to confidently highlight my accomplishments. As my mentor, Janet gave visibility to my successes and provided me with networking opportunities that are rarely afforded to someone with such limited tenure.

My success, coupled with Janet's mentorship, led to two promotions in five years into my first sales leadership position, as I became the youngest manager in the company's history. And not only had I secured these two promotions; I also had two #1 performances in three years. Through Janet's mentorship, I propelled myself to success that most experience only a few times during a decades-long career.

KATE'S GREATEST CHALLENGE

Like all good things, my professional success came to an end, or at least an abrupt standstill. A few years into my leadership role, my company's board replaced the entire executive team. By replacing the executive team, the connections I had spent eight years building—and perhaps more importantly, that Janet had built—evaporated overnight.

I would love to say I immediately recognized the opportunity to highlight my successes and quickly began to add value to the new executive team. Unfortunately, initially I resented the need to reestablish relationships with the new executives. I rejected the notion that I should have to redo the basic work of making the connections necessary for me to provide value to the leadership team, which I had previously built my reputation upon. This led to the greatest challenges of my career (so far).

I now recognize what that months-long funk was: my slow progression through the change cycle. To transition through the doubt and discomfort stages of the change cycle, I evaluated why I had been well respected among my organization's previous leaders and better appreciated Janet's ability to elevate both my accomplishments and me. During my professional career, I had Janet to promote me and my accomplishments throughout the organization. Now, neither of us had these established relationships, so if I was to continue my leadership trajectory, it would become my responsibility to promote myself.

Self-promotion is not something that comes naturally to me, nor to many women. Women rate their performance on average 33% lower than similar-performing men. The December 2019 *Harvard Business Review* article "Why Don't Women Self-Promote as Much" hypothesized that this is because there is a societal backlash when women self-promote, which leads women to weigh the risks of this backlash along with the benefits of self-promotion.

To gain the benefits of self-promotion while mitigating the risk, I began by consistently highlighting my sales representatives' accomplishments to the new executive leadership team. By promoting my team's performance, I was able to establish regular communication with the executive leaders. This became extremely beneficial as my team, and me by extension, became well-known to the leaders. My relationships with the executives were built on the great accomplishments of my team.

Similarly to how Janet elevated me, I highlighted my team to executive leadership. Janet is the kind of leader I will always aspire to be. The person who encourages others, pushes them to believe in themselves, and ensures that when the next opportunity arises, someone on my team is well positioned for the promotion. The mentorship has come full–circle, with twelve of my sales representatives being promoted, thus far.

KATE'S BEST ADVICE

Perhaps because much of my rapid rise to a leadership position is attributed to Janet and her mentorship, it is my responsibility and joy to mentor other women in their careers. Whether or not you are in a leadership role, there are several easy ways you can support your own and other women's career advancements.

The July 2018, *Harvard Business Review* article "Why Women Volunteer for Tasks that Don't Lead to Promotion" revealed that women are far more likely than men to be assigned, as well as volunteer for, nonpromotable tasks. *HBR* defines nonpromotable tasks as "those (tasks) that benefit the organization but don't contribute to the employee's performance evaluation and career advancement." In order for women to ascend to a leadership role, avoiding these nonpromotable tasks is essential so women can instead focus time and energy on high-profile tasks as well as other tasks that contribute to positive evaluations.

Those time-consuming nonpromotable tasks, such as joining your company's party-planning committee, can be obvious. But there are plenty of small, seemingly benign nonpromotable tasks, which combined over time, do not position a woman as a leader. Avoid these small, nonpromotable tasks, which often have a secretarial feel to them, such as taking notes and ordering lunch.

But just as there are small secretarial tasks, there are small tasks that show your initiative and exhibit leadership, enabling you to promote yourself and gain the attention of your organization's leaders. An example of a small initiative task frequently occurs during training sessions, where groups are often formed, each containing a scribe and a presenter. Ensure that you are never the scribe (i.e., secretary); instead, volunteer to be the presenter. As the presenter, you assume a leadership role, not only within your group but also within the entire training class, which often includes leaders from your organization.

Another initiative task includes increasing your participation in meetings. To actively participate in meetings, take a seat at the table, both literally and figuratively. No more sitting along the wall in order to fade into the background. But active participation is not just taking a seat at the table; you must also use your voice by asking and answering questions. By asking and answering questions, you exhibit confidence and knowledge.

If you're a woman already in a leadership position, you have the ability to positively impact the trajectory of other women's careers, regardless of whether or not you are a mentor. Use your leadership position to ensure other women are not placed or volunteer themselves for nonpromotable tasks. When asking for volunteers or assigning nonpromotable tasks, make sure they are equally distributed, just as those high-profile tasks are equally distributed to women as well. And, lastly, don't be afraid to take a risk; your risk can create a life-changing opportunity for someone, just as it did for me.

ABOUT KATE

Kate Fitzgerald is an experienced business development executive, who has spent most of her career cultivating and developing sales teams in order to maximize their potential. One of Kate's biggest accomplishments was becoming the youngest sales manager for the world's second-largest educational technology  company. Kate managed more than seventy sales representatives to award-winning levels of success through her dedication to training, developing, and coaching. Her true passion is for developing the greatest resource: people. Her dedication to sales training and achievement are the reasons for which she is much sought after as a mentor, trainer, and speaker. Kate received her MBA from the University of Louisville as well as two undergraduate degrees from the University of Kentucky.

FIND YOUR VOICE.
FLAUNT YOUR CURLS.

Charanya Kannan
Tech Leader, Speaker, Writer, and Harvard MBA

CHARANYA'S PATH TO LEADERSHIP

My path to leadership has been through experimentation, learning, and pivoting. I used to be a shy child, and when I was in fifth grade, I was given the lead role in a play. After two weeks of rehearsals, they removed me from the lead role because I wasn't loud enough. I didn't accept that decision sitting down. I argued with the drama teacher. I said I would find my voice. But there was no reversal of that decision. I collaborated with another student to create a two-person stand-up comedy on our own. The drama teacher wasn't sure it would be good enough to be selected as a part of the final ensemble. Our performance not only made it to the stage, but it was received by the audience better than the other play. Of course, it helped that in a stand-up comedy I could always stand close to the mike (so I didn't have to be loud). I didn't realize then that I had discovered a way to be successful while being authentic. In high school, I locked myself in a room and shouted out my speech every night, and through that sheer force of grit, I became a debater. Three years later, I didn't need a mike. I subconsciously learned that I could be better at anything by *trying*.

I discovered my love for education when I was fourteen. I changed overnight from the "average" kid to the "top of the class" kid. After that, I have never liked being insignificant or invisible. I made sure my voice was heard and that I could leave a mark behind wherever I went. Despite all that, I was insecure. My initial days of leadership were born more out of a desire to prove myself than out of a passion for change.

Right after my postgraduate study in India, I was hired into the leadership program of one of the largest conglomerates in India. So, at the age of twenty-five, I was sent to Korea on a leadership assignment for a company that the conglomerate had acquired there. I was made the Deputy General Manager within a truck-manufacturing company. I was the only woman to hold a management role there— an Indian woman, at that, who was half the age of her peers, in a new country where age is correlated with power, in an industry flooded with testosterone. I had no idea what to do or how to behave. But I was hungry to prove myself. I picked up learnings and lessons from any corner I could get. That included yelling at others to get my way. (I was explicitly advised to behave that way by a well-meaning mentor, who said I had to stop acting like a polite woman and act like a man to get things done.) I had shed all my identity, trying my best to fit in and be the leader that everyone wanted to see: commanding and temperamental. If I broke some bridges, I was potentially unaware. I experienced sexism along the entire spectrum—all the way from obnoxious passes (tight, inappropriate hugs when I won deals), to explicit misogyny ("If my wife was staying up late like you to finish her office work instead of cooking for me, I'd divorce her"), to subtle, benevolent sexism ("I think of you like my daughter; it is not safe for you to travel to Africa for this deal").

When I presented timelines, I was asked politely how, became pregnant, how it might fit into the plan. Some of these questions were out of genuine curiosity, as their order was challenged for the first time. So I took it in stride. I wasn't even mature enough to understand benevolent sexism at that time; I felt protected instead. But the incremental weight of all of this gradually accumulated, and I could feel the heaviness pound in my chest.

Eventually, I applied to Harvard Business School and moved to the West. It finally felt glorious to be among people who got me. I learned new terms that helped define situations and how I felt about those. Ah, the joy of discovering the lexicon that mitigates feelings of loneliness as you discover your tribe! It made me realize how much youthful energy I had spent so far in waging uphill gender battles. Starting as a leader at a young age can sound glamorous, but if given a chance, I'd want to work my way upward. I navigated negotiations and political battles with ease but couldn't build a simple model in an Excel sheet or write a polite email without sounding like I was trying to harass the recipient. I didn't feel like an imposter; I *knew* I was an imposter. I decided to reset my career and start from scratch because I understood that leadership was less about power and more about abilities. And I wanted to build solid abilities. I took up strategic consulting, which was an excellent ground for getting trained in basic managerial abilities. And after that, I moved to my current role at PayPal, where I'm helping drive customer centricity globally. It took me a few years of introspection to understand my authentic self. And now I'm focusing on bringing that authentic self to work every day, focusing on the work and not my gender, focusing on leading through goodwill and not through a girdle.

CHARANYA'S GREATEST CHALLENGE

It might seem like gender barriers were some of my greatest hurdles initially. Perhaps that was so, but in my head, I would think my greatest barriers were internal: the voices in my head that would occasionally tell me I can't do it. A friend's mother asked me when I was sixteen if I intended to apply to IITs, the best engineering colleges in India. I laughed and said, "Why would I apply there? I'm a girl," and if I could go back and slap my sixteen-year-old self, I would do that.

A lot of the challenges I have overcome in my leadership path have been internal. I believed I wasn't good at math. There was no one to tell me I was actually good at it, and I simply lacked the confidence to display it. I didn't have an identity as I moved from country to country. In a quest to be accepted and then successful, I'd camouflage myself into the surroundings, becoming a mirror that reflected anything that was thrown at me. I'd quickly get distracted by every goal and aspiration, trying to be everything to everyone. It took a lot of reflection, sharing, and being vulnerable and open to change that led me down a fruitful path. Over the past few years, I have tried to ground myself in who I really am. I have a stronger grasp of what my strengths and interests are, which battles I am willing to wage, and which ones I want to stay away from. I have also realized that introspection and being in tune with myself are not a goal but a habit—one that enables me to be emotionally grounded. I've realized that my ambition shouldn't be like a finish line at the Olympics, which signifies victory when crossed, but it is a subtle feeling of satisfaction of having done my best each day.

CHARANYA'S BEST ADVICE

A good leader must have three things: expertise in the topic, confidence, and accountability.

No, actually not. I don't believe in ascribing the qualities of a leader. For centuries and decades, there was a stereotype and mold for what leadership is. This dates back to a primitive time, where the oldest, most vociferous male was made head of the tribe.

And then we got to a time when leadership was all about the powerful warrior, the one who could slay the most men, ruthlessly kill women and children, succeed in battles and combats—the world where Napoleon was glorified. The smart, intelligent ones were often only the advisors. It wasn't until the Industrial Revolution and the evolution of the modern state that leadership began to evolve, when the smartest statesman began to rule. With the advent of democracy, the most popular leader—the one who could market himself well, talk to a crowd or gathering, understand the voter base—was the new kind of leader to emerge.

What was happening on the business front? Something similar, as Henry Ford's leadership style took hold, which was demonstrated by his assurance that a customer could have a car of any color—as long as it was black.

It is only in the past fifty years that feminist movements have started to spark a debate, and we now have more women leaders, more diversity. We are moving away from molds and stereotypical notions of what a leader should look and behave like. If you look at leadership courses from fifteen years ago, they prescribed certain methods, such as appearing taller, projecting confidence, learning to throw your voice. I don't believe in such advice because any advice like that means only that we are lending ourselves to a stereotype.

And that is when I came across the single most important leadership advice, called *authenticity*. Authenticity is so powerful to me because it means we are moving away from stereotypes where people project and pretend to be someone they're not, just because they want to be a leader. Often, when you project yourself like that but don't feel true to it, you feel like an imposter. When you don't believe in yourself, there is a cognitive dissonance, and then no one will believe in you.

And what does authenticity mean? It means you have to think about who you really are, including what matters the most to you and what style of leadership is important to you. That also means that different contexts require different leaders: the leadership needed to run a household is different from the local school leadership, which is different from management or military or national leadership. So instead of giving advice on what a leader should look like, let me talk more about my leadership journey.

In Korea, I was told I'd have to wear makeup to be taken seriously. I outrightly refused, and I still don't wear it. I used to think that people with curls could never be leaders; now I'm embracing it. I used to think people of my height (5'3") couldn't be a leader; now I think I can. I used to think people with my accent couldn't be a leader; now I think I can. I am frank and outspoken, and although I've learned diplomacy, I've left organizations that required me to be overtly diplomatic. I know exactly what my strengths are. I know that learning constantly is important for me. Being challenged is important for me. I've come to realize that emotional stability is really important. Being able to understand that all of us are humans and understanding how to help others channel their emotions well while also trying to understand my own emotions without them interfering in decision making is critical. And I'm trying to work towards that. Most of all, I'm trying to lead without expectations except for giving my best each day. I found my voice, and I flaunt my curls.

ABOUT CHARANYA

Charanya Kannan leads Global Consumer Insights and Strategy within PayPal. Charanya has an MBA from Harvard Business School, where she graduated with honors, and also has degrees in Marketing and Engineering. She has close to ten years of experience in Strategy and Operations, working across multiple geographies, such as India, South Korea, and the United States. She was previously with the leadership program of the Tata group in India and Korea, where she was the youngest woman and the only woman to hold a leadership role in the 2500+ company. She drove their international strategy, resulting in the company's expansion across geographies. She is a classically trained corporate strategist, as she spent two years at the prestigious management consulting firm BCG.

Charanya is passionate about gender equality and is pushing the boundaries internally within PayPal and externally. While at Harvard, she was the Vice President of the Women's Association and a writer for the campus magazine, *Harbus*. She invests time to train her team on critical skills, such as fostering psychological safety, nurturing diversity of opinion, and using behavioral economics to drive customer outcomes. She mentors young business students by establishing relationships between universities and PayPal and by creating strategic projects for students and personally spending time guiding them. She has been featured in *Business Insider, Times of India, The News Minute*, and most recently, she made it onto the list of fifty most influential people by *Chennai Insider*.

Outside of PayPal, she is a facilitator for Harvard Circles (a program to foster relationships among women) and is a speaker at several events on topics of consumer centricity, gender, and behavioral economics. She is a mentor at the Cherie Blair Foundation, mentoring women in running e-commerce businesses.

SHOW UP BOLDLY, CONFIDENTLY, AND UNAPOLOGETICALLY

Shanté R. Roddy
CEO, She Epic Media; Host, She Boss Talk

SHANTÉ'S PATH TO LEADERSHIP

It's hard to chronicle my exact path to leadership because as far back as I can remember, I've always been a leader. When I say I've always been a leader, what I mean is that I've always been drawn to leadership roles. My path to leadership, therefore, has been pretty linear. I've hopped from one leadership position to the next until I landed in the one I have now. So I'd like to say I've had more than thirty years of leadership experience.

During my time at school, I took on several leadership roles. For example, I was the editor/co-editor for the newspaper. I even took on leadership roles in gym class. I got a letter jacket due to my support of the coach/gym teacher. I also credit my work with school counselors as being an important part of my leadership journey. Working with school counselors equipped me with access to a lot of opportunities, which helped me to empower other people by giving them access to these opportunities. Today, exposing other people to opportunities forms an integral part of my own business, so it has all come full circle.

My attraction to leadership roles continued into adulthood. Before I became a full-time entrepreneur, I held management positions in corporate America.

I am not in a space right now where I could ever go back to corporate America. While my experience there sharpened my leadership skill and was an important part of my journey, my vision, my dreams, and my purpose are too big to be limited by that system. I just need the space and the room to be able to fulfill my purpose and my mission, which is to help women dominate the decade.

Certain core values and characteristics have led me to my current leadership position as the CEO of She Epic Media and the host of She Boss Talk. First of all, I've always been a disruptor. I view being a disruptor as a positive thing because through disruption we can effect much-needed change. I was a disruptor in my last leadership role because I'm of the mindset that if it's not working, let's change it. Let's always be working towards improvement. I've done this for every company for which I've worked. I was able to set up and change a whole quality system, an entire project management office department. I was able to go into a company and change the housing system and work with HUD. Taking on leadership roles allowed me to implement new systems and enforce new policies. In addition to that, I was tasked with making sure that the team knew all the systems and were versed in all the policies so that we could roll them out across the board. Whatever capacity I'm working in, I'm usually taking on a leadership role and usually working in multiple roles as a leader.

Other qualities that have helped me find the leadership position I now hold are being dependable and reliable, and taking initiative. I've also always had a purpose for everything. In terms of a job, I know that I will take initiative and not just do what the job description says verbatim. Taking initiative, trying to see where there is the most need for my knowledge, expertise, wisdom, and leadership—that has really helped me in the leadership roles that I've served in over the years, including the one I have now.

Finally, I'd say my resilience and my willingness to chart different paths have prepared me for my leadership roles.

SHANTÉ'S GREATEST CHALLENGE

Leadership has been a road of challenges and successes. I think one of my greatest challenges as a leader is being visible when I didn't want to be visible. As a leader, a true leader, you're put on the front lines and tasked with making the tough decisions. Unfortunately, that means you get hurt a lot. By the time I exited corporate America, I had been through so much. In my eyes, I was doing the right thing, but being visible left me exposed and open to sabotage and other negativity.

People really do intentionally try to sabotage you as a leader. I've experienced this many times. I'm naturally a collaborative person and a big believer in the power of collaboration. I actively advocate for entrepreneurs and women coming together to collaborate and partner. Of course, I take a leadership role in those efforts to collaborate. Unfortunately, it doesn't always work out, even though I've made several attempts to do so. For example, people have taken my vision or idea as their own.

I've addressed and overcome not wanting to be visible and not wanting to experience sabotage by being courageous. Despite the fact that there might be forces trying to stop you from doing what you know is right as a leader, don't let that stop you. Be acutely aware that you cannot please everybody as a leader, but simultaneously be confident in your decision-making. With regard to the sabotage, understand it can happen, and know you just have to be able to move forward. Do not let that circumstance or that particular situation affect relationships going forward. Being able to put yourself out there despite knowing the fact these painful situations could happen is courageous in itself.

SHANTÉ'S BEST ADVICE

The best advice I would give to a woman in leadership or who is ascending into a leadership role is to be confident. Women, especially in this time, have to show up boldly, confidently, and unapologetically as the women that we are. We have to take center stage, and that means coming out from the shadows. It's not easy, but this is a challenge that I know many other women besides me deal with in their careers.

One way for women to be more confident is to recognize their uniqueness and to show up authentically. That's a challenge for a lot of people because they feel like they need to fit in. You have to make peace with the fact that while you need or want to be likable, not everyone is going to like you. However, I think if women show up authentically as who they are, that is going to be very important to being a leader. It helps because people can sense when you're wearing a mask and hiding your true self. People are drawn to and respect authenticity.

In addition to that, if we as women want to be leaders, we have to take our place. So many of us are leaders, but we're leaders from the background, in the shadows. Prioritize visibility. We all know that there are barriers out there, but we have to push through and take our opportunity by force if that's what it takes.

I'd like to add that it's important to play on your strengths and not use your weaknesses as excuses. For example, if you're an introvert, large crowds may not work for you; they definitely don't for me. However, you know that forming relationships by networking is a very important part of business and leadership. Leaders have to be able to develop and manage relationships; there is no way around that. One thing I've done is to seek out people for one-on-one meetings, whether virtually or in person. I've also had to decide that I was going to overcome the challenge of being visible and making connections. My advice is to decide that you're going to overcome all obstacles and play on your strengths to do so.

Finally, everybody's path to leadership is different. What you'll find in common with most of the paths are a willingness to be open and have enough courage to step into a leadership role. You have to be intentional and decisive. Start where you are and go forward.

ABOUT SHANTÉ

Shanté R. Roddy is a mastermind, disruptor of the status quo, master collaborator, and advocate for women. Her desire is to see all women WIN! Her motto is We're Better Together!

Shanté is the founder and CEO of She Epic Media and host of She Boss Talk, an international talk show, podcast, blog, and network. At She Epic Media, the team shines the spotlight on businesswomen and their gifts, stories, and voices to educate, empower, and elevate women to dream bigger and live bigger.

Shanté is an event producer, who teaches other women to leverage events to elevate their platform, take center stage, and go from hunter to hunted when it comes to attracting and converting their ideal clients. Under She Epic Conference, Shanté hosts and cohosts a number of events, including her signature event, She Boss Extravaganza.

She is proud to lead an online network of over 20,000 women in business, facilitating several initiatives and events to bring us together, break barriers, and create opportunities for collaboration and success.

Shanté's mission is helping purpose-driven women entrepreneurs increase their influence, impact, and income to give them more time, results, and freedom to live life without limits. I am SHE!

FIND A GAP IN YOUR INDUSTRY AND RUN WITH IT

Sarah Yeverovich
Co-Founder

SARAH'S PATH TO LEADERSHIP

I did not always want to be an entrepreneur. When I was younger, I was not sure what I wanted to be. I liked working with people, I liked engaging with different personalities, I was always very outgoing, and I knew I wanted to do something within the sales realm.

When I graduated from college, I worked for a multibillion-dollar publishing company, and after working there for eight years, I had learned a lot but wanted to take on a new challenge. I worked my way up in the company to become sales rep of the year at the organization, and being in the company's employ was an amazing experience; but I was craving more and wanted to change my career. I noticed the world making the shift to online selling of eBooks instead of print editions. The early 2000s saw an acceleration in the digital shift, and digital marketing was on the rise; I found it fascinating and wanted to take advantage of that.

At the time, my brother was in the recruiting world and had helped an organization that started with fewer than five employees grow to become an Inc 1000 firm. He then decided to go off and recruit on his own. Since I was also in the market for a new challenge, I decided to take a risk, learn to recruit, and partner with him. Partnering in 2011, we slowly but surely became the experts in digital marketing, eCommerce, and tech recruiting.

We have grown our firm year after year and now have an amazing team of executive recruiters, researchers, and business-development professionals; we took a risk and it paid off. I believe when you are passionate about what you do, it translates to the client that you really care and that you share the client's best interest. In recruiting, you are dealing with people, not selling a product. We take pride in what we do, and because of our results in finding above-market talent, over 95% of our business is repeat and referral business and our clients feel that we are an extended arm of their company. My team, my brother, and I love what we do; we get joy out of walking into companies and seeing the people we hire and the success they are having.

Life also throws you unexpected opportunities. Just as I was finally feeling that I had a handle on our recruiting business and was starting to scale up, we started another venture, RecruiterPM. My firm had found a gap in the recruiting market. We incorporated AI, project management, analytics, and customer relationship management to make a powerful recruiting software application. I was constantly searching for an easy-to-use trackable system to measure employee metrics, spend, clients, and other things that I could link or use with my applicant-tracking system. When I discovered there was nothing that was simple to use or that had all the features I was looking for, we decided to create the software ourselves, for our own use. When we then spoke with other recruiters about what we had created, we found that they too had some of our pain points and could not find a good, simple system that was specific to recruiting. Over the past year, we hired a team and perfected our system, with plans to launch in 2021. I am very excited by this new venture that unexpectedly came about, and it just shows that you never know what the future might hold. If you have a good idea, find a gap in your industry and run with it!

SARAH'S GREATEST CHALLENGE

For me, the main thing I always try to be mindful of is to slow down and live in the moment. Being fast-paced, I need to remind myself of this all the time.

Additionally, I am always working on how to best manage different people and personalities. I have a coach who helps me with issue/problem processing, I read a lot, and I constantly learn from others. I made some mistakes early on in my company, but I learned and grew from those events. It's not about how you think people should be managed; it's about really getting to know your team and learn what leadership style will make them thrive based on their personalities. A strong leader should have empathy and take the time to know and understand the people they work with. Set goals and be clear with everyone on expectations. There is no one-size-fits-all approach for leadership, which is why leadership is difficult and something on which most people, including myself, are constantly working.

SARAH'S BEST ADVICE

When you are hiring, you want to make sure that you are hiring someone not only for their hard skills but for their soft skills as well and that they embody and line up with your company's core values. It is also important for you to trust your employees, and for them to trust you. Be patient and always set goals, and from the beginning, be clear with everyone on expectations. If your employees do not know what your expectations are, then you will not be aligned and might not hit your goals.

A lot of people ask me, "What are some top tips for things to do during an interview?" Here are some things I have found work well to help you get the best feel for someone during an interview and make the best hiring decision:

Have more of a conversational interview. This really helps you get to know someone, their style, and soft skills. Interviewing is not a natural, everyday thing for most people. When you have an engaging conversation and ask open-ended questions, you tend to get more out of the interview, rather than just throwing questions at a candidate. Being bombarded with questions can also make more passively seeking candidates feel that they are being interrogated rather than trying to get to know them and giving them a better understanding of the position and company.

Asking good questions throughout your conversation is half the battle. Before you start the interview process, think about things that are important for you in each role and formulate questions that will give you the best insight. If an answer from a candidate does not make sense, do not hesitate to dive deeper. It is better to address concerns right away than to leave the interview wondering.

If you are a manager conducting an interview for a new role or a role you are not an expert in, do not be scared to have a candidate elaborate on an answer if it does not make sense to you. An expert in a certain area should be able to explain one's area of expertise in a way that non-specialists can understand.

Include questions that directly link to your core values. If someone has the right hard skills but is not a cultural fit, then the candidate may not be ideal for a long-lasting hire.

Lastly, make sure things match up. Take notes during the interview. If there is a point into which you want to dig deeper or an express that gives you some reservation or that just doesn't add up, ask it again in a different way in the second interview and make sure the candidate's reply is in line with what he or she previously said.

If you are the person interviewing or conducting the interview, honesty and transparency are crucial intangibles that must be established from the beginning. If anyone on either side is misleading, it will make for the wrong hire. Be open and honest about what you, the position, and the organization can do for the candidate so that you set-up yourself for success. If you don't know that answer to something, say so! Employers should be real about what is expected and should communicate clear goals for each role for which they are hiring.

ABOUT SARAH

Sarah Yeverovich co-founded Empowered Staffing in 2012, and her team of Executive Recruiters specialize in digital marketing, eCommerce, SaaS, Technology, and healthcare recruitment. Besides running Empowered Staffing, Sarah is a proud wife and mother of three.

REIGN YOUR LANE

Esther Renee
The People's CHRO^{SM}

ESTHER'S PATH TO LEADERSHIP

CONTRIBUTION SIGNIFICANCE. Of all I had scribbled on that sheet of paper, these two words were speaking to my soul's yearning. Entering a new season, I realized it was time to take another leap and move on in my career journey. Sometimes we simply must move on. Make no mistake: every position I'd ever taken represented upward mobility, a new challenge, and greater responsibility—and I was grateful. Job titles of positions held in chronological order were Representative, Coordinator, Supervisor, Assistant Administrator, Manager, and Adjunct Professor. One after another—be it in academia, in the workplace, as well as through projects, serving on boards, or involved in extracurricular activities—I'd been afforded opportunities to grow professionally and personally. There followed increased decision making, more direct reports, increased budgetary accountability, greater visibility, and my name discussed among leadership. Those at the C-suite level were beginning to know me and my work. Nevertheless, something was missing. No matter how much I did, the one thing missing was the feeling—no, in fact, the knowledge—that the work I did was truly something that mattered.

There I was, creating a list of "must-haves" and "deal breakers" for my next career move. This is an activity I encourage many of my coaching clients and mentees to do regarding their various life decisions. I had several offers on the table, and I knew this next position would be the pivot point. Sure, I wrote all the expected and desired characteristics for someone pursuing a leadership role—personal and organization mission alignment, autonomy, great pay and benefits, empowerment, challenging work, collaborative leadership team—and I listed a few other key factors. However, when I wrote the words CONTRIBUTION SIGNIFICANCE, I knew they were symbolic of so much more. It was a point of demarcation between a good or great career move. And it instantly became my priority #1.

I declined the offers on the table and continued the search for a position where CONTRIBUTION SIGNIFICANCE would be desired and celebrated. My contemplations of disappointment, such as, "I would have done 'X'," or "Why aren't they listening," or "I wish leadership would get it together," helped to fill my personal leadership journal. It included a transformative list of practical dos and don'ts for when I finally assumed a new position—a role where I would see policies, processes, procedures, and products that I authored or on which I led the charge to impact both the internal and external customers positively. Through walking in a well-defined leadership style and networking with confidence without changing the core dynamics of who I am and what I have to offer, I earned the position as a Chief Human Resources Officer. Through clarity, focus, and diligence, opportunity placed me in front of a CEO who recognized I was the missing component to the organization's leadership team, and my CONTRIBUTION SIGNIFICANCE would be honored.

ESTHER'S GREATEST CHALLENGE

Navigating interpersonal relationships with peers and subordinates in any environment—but especially with those in the workforce who demonstrate an inability to judge what is right and wrong and thus act accordingly—has been one of my greatest challenges as a leader and human resources professional. Our world is filled with all types of individuals, and I've encountered the full range in the workplace, from the exceptional to the average to the reprehensible. That's humanity; everywhere we look we will find a mixture of problems, perspectives, personalities, and penchants that contribute to how people perform. Being a leader presents me with an opportunity to "lead" each. But how do you deal with the one thing for which you admit you personally lack tolerance? For me, the intentional corrupt, unethical, and immoral are cancerous to all that is good and salvageable where we worship, work, live, and play. How does one honor the humanity of an individual who moves throughout the work environment with questionable morals, ethics, and integrity? How does one perceive humanity's fallibility, especially in the area of ethics, yet simultaneously honor that individual with the necessary grace and tolerance?

Both personal and professional experiences support my assertion that there are several common contributors to the pervasion of those challenged in the areas of governing themselves well while lacking sound moral practices. I have found the most significant contributors are low competency, organizational politics, situational ethics, and society modeling the way.

At times, people just don't have the knowledge, skills, or abilities—better known as competencies—to do the right thing. As the adage goes, "People do what they know." A grace-filled perspective allows me to acknowledge that some people may not know what is right in a particular circumstance. I maximize this type of situation as an opportunity to inform and educate.

Within many organizations, a big-P and small-p struggle occurs; sometimes it is the unspoken rule of thumb: politics. Whether decisions are made to conform with local, state, or federal government–based pressures (big P) or to increase personal status or power positioning (small p), neither fair well. I combat this unavoidable issue by finding an opportunity during my employment interview to express my unwavering principle to not play the politics game. I would prefer not to get hired by an organization desiring my political game-playing compliance than to be forced to prove true to my word by not fulfilling any false expectations to participate in the big-P and small-p struggle. I simply will not.

Some practice a form of self-serving situational ethics. Whatever will serve their best interest is what they do, focused more on the benefit and less on what is right. Unfortunately, I have found some people losing sight of their ethics, the further up the leadership ladder they climb. Imagine having crucial conversations with fellow C-suite members about sensitive topics such as responsibility, accountability, professionalism, trust, mutual respect, and moral character. This is one of the truest tests of a leader, The Abilene Paradox, which challenges whether one should go along to get along or stick to individual knowledge of doing what is best and, in this case, right.

Lastly, we don't have to look far to see how society can and does impact workplace culture. Just turn on the news. As a human resources professional, I witness and combat how the degradation of society in holding people accountable for their bad behavior has transferred into the mindset of much of the workforce. While it can be very challenging, even contentious, refusing to do as the world does and rather holding firm to integrity has become my mainstay, even if it costs me workplace relationships. By being in a leadership role, leading by example is my modus operandi.

The solution to this ethics conundrum is like walking a tightrope and not falling off by maintaining a balance between justice and grace. But how? Justice? Grace? Justice? Grace? Too much of one without the other will cause us to come tumbling down, every time. And if you haven't noticed, the higher the leadership role, the further one has to fall. The ultimate required competency is possessing a strong aptitude for fairness. I have found that my proclivity for justice is innate. Perhaps it is part of my personality design and part learned behavior as a component of my chosen profession; regardless, I enjoy the process of right being triumphant. I employ my faith-based wisdom and my mediation and arbitration skills, and I rely on strong policy design and administration to advocate for what is right. My main objective is for the people who've encountered me in their process of receiving justice to don objective lenses and, thereby, acknowledge that I, above all, honored their humanity without losing sight of what's right!

ESTHER'S BEST ADVICE

Reign your lane! Daily, you engage in the process of becoming exactly who you are designed to be. The itinerary features magnificent wins and sometimes disappointing losses. The hard-earned milestones and the life-shifting lessons learned send you down roadways filled with road signs, traffic lights, and at times detours. The challenges overcome, changes embraced, and character built become the on-ramp to an expressway to your destined success. All of your life experiences, educational pursuits, and professional endeavors make it easy to merge into the lane that will allow you to travel unencumbered; this is your lane!

But what exactly do you need to do to reign your lane?

Be sure to map your trek before starting. I like to chart several alternate routes just in case something takes me off course. Define for yourself how you'd like to get to your destination, as you know there are multiple ways to get to the same endpoint. Additionally, make note of how far you'll get with the fuel you have. It is equally important to know when you'll need to stop for a refill. Good leaders practice strategic planning to ensure that their resources and priorities align with achieving their goals and that they will get where they are headed on time, within budget, and with excellence.

Finding your way to this place that few truly find for themselves should be your main objective. This is the most important thing you can do to ensure your quest for leadership is achieved. Conversely, don't forget to enjoy the journey and take note of important mile markers found along the way. What speed feels comfortable to you? What landmarks are important for you? Make sure they are included in your journey. While following behind another person—woman or man—who has made it to a place similar to where you want to go is an option, going your own way is invigorating and rewarding. Roll down the window and allow the wind to blow in your face, keeping you aware and awake. Adjust your rear-view mirror, but remember that strong leaders will not focus on the past or the previous wrong turns made; instead, they look ahead with a clear focus on upcoming opportunities. The rear-view mirror is great to help keep you mindful of tailgaters and perhaps most importantly, to check your lipstick.

There are several warnings to heed. First because you are not the only one traveling the highway to leadership, make note that both road hazards and potholes may have been created, and doing all you can to avoid them is wise. Second, equip yourself with all-weather tires because as a leader you will need to be able to navigate every possible weather condition. The correct tools will make what challenges others very easy for you. Third, as mentioned, there will be others on the road. That's okay. Share the road and allow them to pass when necessary and avoid bad behavior like road rage. If you observe another driver experiencing difficulty, consider stopping to help them if at all possible. All too often we become too focused on ourselves that we forget our peers. However, if one is in another lane and is taking a different route, remember the lane you are in and stay focused. If you focus on them you may find yourself swerving and getting off track.

At a certain point, you will recognize the smooth road and the ease as you traverse. Your journey doesn't have to be inordinately difficult and once you are in the correct lane, put on your cruise control, sit back and enjoy it as you Reign Your Lane!

ABOUT ESTHER

Esther Renee is a C-suite Servant Leader, Visionary, Human Resources Professional, Multipassionate "Ministerpreneur," Freedom Facilitator and Pageantista!

Professional certifications achieved, academic degrees attained, communities served, career ladders climbed and glass ceilings broken—Esther Renee is the Chief Human Resources Officer for a global cyber, site, and personal identity security company. Concurrently, she uses diverse gifts as a multipassionate "Ministerpreneur." Professional experiences in public, private, nonprofit, and small business sectors contribute to over twenty-five years' experience in human resources, quality, and project management. Yet and still, her greatest purpose in life is achieved as she helps others REACH Freedom from life experiences, traumas, and choices that have placed them in bondage. She accomplishes this through the use of deliverance and healing ministry techniques for the spirit, soul, and body.

Just like her namesake in the Bible, it's only fitting that Esther is destined to wear a crown. From the adrenaline rush of her first pageant in 8th grade to also participating in dance, theatre, and modeling, she soon realized that performing arts and pageantry contributed to overcoming self-esteem challenges. She was set on pace to walk confidently into her platform, passion, and purpose.

A lover of all things pageantry, Esther has participated in local, state, and national pageants while focusing on promoting her perpetual platform of engaging, educating, and empowering females in all things Self-Esteem. In 2006, she launched the "Be yoU... Do yoU...Love yoU!" (BUDULU) brand, which further led to her founding the BUDULU Foundation, a nonprofit organization providing support for self-esteem related research and initiatives.

Esther is a dedicated advocate for women's issues as exemplified through both her entrepreneurial and community service initiatives. She served on a global level while being the chapter leader for Days for Girls (Columbus) and continues to serve the organization as a certified Women's Health Ambassador. Days for Girls increases access to menstrual care and education by developing global partnerships, cultivating social enterprises, mobilizing volunteers, and innovating sustainable solutions that shatter stigmas and limitations for women and girls, particularly in developing countries.

For fun and relaxation, Esther Renee spends time with family and friends, interprets dreams, creates paper beads (it's a thing), cloud gazes (#skeyecandy #headintheclouds), and watches stand-up comics and nature shows.

LIVE YOUR LIFE OUT LOUD

Michelle Elizabeth Brown
Public Speaker, Author, and Activist

MICHELLE'S PATH TO LEADERSHIP

In my family/community, I was always influenced by strong, powerful women taking leadership roles. You might even say it is in my DNA. My paternal great-grandmother and grandmother were known in their hometown of Henderson, Kentucky, as the women you went to for help. They taught children and adults to read and write and advocated for their community's well-being. I learned that my paternal grandfather had been instrumental in starting the first NAACP branch in their town. My maternal grandparents' home in Detroit was known as the go-to place for a meal and a place for shelter. My godmother registered people to vote. As a child, I was always watching, learning, and helping.

I developed a reintegration/training program for women at risk (victims of domestic violence, homelessness, substance abuse, etc.) to help them develop life skills. And while working with a nonprofit housing corporation, I planned and developed affordable housing projects in urban areas. I was instilled with a dedication to helping the community, individuals, and organizations develop, grow, and use their own unique force.

What moved me from being one of the crew to a leadership role came at a brunch sponsored by the Human Rights Campaign. The keynote speaker was an African-American woman whose son had been brutally murdered. I was one of only a handful of people of color in the audience and the only African-American woman. After her remarks, we talked, and she asked me "Where were our people?" She then challenged me to be present, to step up and be that voice at the table, and then bring others with me. Her words were powerful and hit me hard. I realized that my life experience as an African-American woman in the LGBTQ community gave me a voice that could create change in my many intersectional communities.

After that conversation, I joined the Michigan steering committee. As an elected member of the Board of Governors, I traveled to Washington, DC, and challenged my fellow governors to do more than talk about diversity and inclusion. I left that meeting as Co-chair of the National Diversity Community.

At the heart of all the work I have done is my love of helping those on the fringes of society. I have volunteered for many organizations, assisting those who often go unheard in society. I have served on the board of directors for several organizations. Social injustice, diversity, fairness for women, youth, and people of color are areas receiving a great deal of my time and effort.

I have also used my voice to inspire and lead as a writer for area newspapers and as a public speaker.

MICHELLE'S GREATEST CHALLENGE

My greatest challenge has been standing for truth in situations where others would prefer to keep me in a box or define my narrative for me, to be authentic and hold space, channeling my righteous indignation in the most difficult of situations so as not to suck all the air out of the room or take a scorched-earth approach, to be a catalyst for new or collaborative ideas/action— not always easy!

In some spaces, I am known as a poet. Often when I am tapped for a speaking engagement, the host is expecting more traditional, "rosy" poetry and is surprised when I step to the mic with poems like "A Prayer for True Colors," which pushes for true diversity and inclusion; "I Don't Need Your Words to Tell My Story," which tells a story of Black literacy, often dismissed; and "I Vote Because," which reflects upon the civil rights struggle. One of my favorites is "Don't Touch My Hair," with its reminder that ...

> My hair tells the story of Mother Africa Strong, Black and Proud
> Some curls tell stories of bondage rape and humiliation,
> While the kink speaks of struggle and resilience.

As a speaker, I stand boldly in the crosshairs of my intersectionality and come prepared to speak for social justice. Being an African-American woman who is also a member of the LGBTQ community does not limit me; it empowers me. I sometimes find it necessary to remind others that I have a place at the table for Black Lives Matter, not only as a Black woman, but as a mother of a young Black man and on behalf of our transgender community. I have a place at the Women's Rights table, not only as a woman, but to talk about the economic disparity in general for women—especially for women of color—reproductive rights and taking our power to the polls.

I have thoughts on and a voice for all of my communities—young, old, Black/White/POC, and LGBTQ. To borrow from Sojourner Truth's speech—"Ain't I a Woman?" Yes, I am, and I will not be defined by your narrative!

MICHELLE'S BEST ADVICE

Recognize your power! You are stronger than you may realize, which is why you face resistance. Listen to other voices. Collaborate and build sisterhood. We are often pitted against one another, but we don't have to play that game. If you have access to a resource or information and share it with your sister, it does not make you weaker. It makes all of us stronger. It doesn't mean we all have to stand around, holding hands, singing kumbaya. Some will, some won't; but as we share resources and information, we will all progress, even if not on the same path.

Remember, you are paving the way for young women, girls, and boys who will come up behind you. If each generation has to reinvent the wheel, we will stay in the same rut. Lead by example by living your life out loud. You never know who is watching. Think about it: besides the obvious role models in your life, wasn't there someone you saw, maybe just in passing, who influenced you? Someone you looked at and said, "That's who I want to be like" or "I can do that"? BE THAT WOMAN! BE THAT PERSON! You never know who is watching—a girl, a boy, maybe even another woman who just needs a little inspiration.

Here's my favorite story: While attending an event/meeting for Vice President Biden in 2014, one of the agents checking IDs looked at me and said, "You probably don't remember me, but I saw you speak. And I thought 'if that Black woman can stand up before this room of White men and speak her truth, then I can stand in mine.'" BE THAT WOMAN! BE THAT PERSON!

Your words have power; speak wisely; share your stories. The good, bad, and ugly: these are life lessons. Make memories, make history. Be that welcomed breath of fresh air, that cosmic breeze filling space with hope, love, and ideas. And when things don't go quite the way you want, don't give up: listen, learn, and adjust your course.

Never forget that in your very existence YOU ARE POWERFUL!

ABOUT MICHELLE

Two words to describe public speaker, author, and activist Michelle Elizabeth Brown are "a force."

She was born and raised in Detroit, graduating from Cass Technical High School, then went on to attend Wayne State University.

Through her career, creative endeavors, and volunteer work, she has used her strength to assist, inspire, and move the community, individuals, and organizations to be the best they can be. Mixed with her desire to help others, she also finds her dedication to uplifting those often left on the fringe of society, especially women, people of color, and the LGBTQ community.

Michelle has worked as a consultant to small businesses, nonprofit organizations, and individuals in the areas of accounting, business management, and marketing.

The force within Michelle is her voice, and as a public speaker and activist, she has used her voice to educate, inform, and uplift diverse groups of people in a variety of areas.

She was one of the speakers at the 2017 Women's March in Ann Arbor, MI, and returned in 2018 and 2019 as the main speaker at Ann Arbor's Women's March.

As a guest lecturer in the role of artist/activist at universities, various pride celebrations, and social justice forums, and in hosting her national weekly internet radio show "Collections by Michelle Brown," Michelle consistently illustrates the need to build up all individuals within a community in order to strengthen the entire community.

Michelle developed a reintegration/training program for women at risk (victims of domestic violence, homelessness, substance abuse, etc.) to help them develop life skills. And while working with a nonprofit housing corporation, she planned and developed affordable housing projects in urban areas.

She has served on the board of directors of the Ruth Ellis Center, Affirmations, National Black Justice Coalition, and Michigan Equality. She also served on the Board of Governors of the Human Rights Campaign, co-chairing the organization's National Diversity Committee.

She served as Interim Executive Director of the Cass Corridor Neighborhood Development Corp. and Co-Executive Director of Michigan Equality prior to its merger with The Triangle Foundation.

She uses the force of her words as a writer for area newspapers and is a regular columnist for Between the Lines newspaper. She has written two books of poetry and a children's book. She is a regular guest on the Bayard Rustin Center for Social Justice Power Hour in Princeton, NJ, the Esteem Awards in Chicago, IL, and ZAMI Nobla in Atlanta, GA.

Michelle's force is also found within her desire to give. She has volunteered for many organizations, assisting those that often go unheard in society. Social injustice, diversity, and fairness for women, youth, and people of color are areas that receive a great deal of her time and effort.

In the past ten years, Michelle has been recognized and awarded for the work she does within the community. Both the National Congress of Black Women (Oakland County, Michigan) and the Department of Veterans Affairs (Saginaw, Michigan) recognized her in 2016, and others have recognized her for her tireless work to support, inspire, and elevate people and communities including the following:

Women in Leadership Award Nominee, 2020

Transforming Power Fund Community Table, 2019

Panelist NAACP National-State of POC LGBTQ, 2019

Media Sponsor Award, Lupus Detroit, 2019

Community Ally Award, Black Trans Advocacy Inc, 2016

The G-List Black LGBTQ Influencer, 2015

Esteem Award Outstanding Blog Radio Can We Talk For Real,
2014

Esteem Award Outstanding Service Female—National, 2012

Inductee Who's Who in Black Detroit, 2011

OUT Magazine Hidden 100 LGBT POC Leaders, 2011

Media Award—Michigan Annual Pride Banquet, 2007

Award of Merit National Poetry Society, 2007

Triangle Foundation Catalyst Award, 2005

Spirit of Detroit Award, 2005

Diversity Outreach Award—Human Rights Campaign,
2004–2006

TAKE TEAMS WHERE THEY DO NOT REALIZE THEY WANT TO GO

Juliet Kasaya
Senior Corporate Trainer

JULIET'S PATH TO LEADERSHIP

I started my career as a pharmacy technician on a clinical team at a call center. I was fresh out of college and trying to figure out my next move. Like many new grads, I had a plan. I was going to work while applying to go to grad school, so I was not ready to settle into a career quite yet. Little did I know that my path was going to change faster than I had imagined. We were in the midst of an acquisition, and my leaders saw something in me that I hadn't quite identified. I found myself training individuals and leading a team. I often tell people that leadership does not need permission.

Wherever you are, you can lead, and oftentimes this is how leaders are identified.

Back to business as usual, our team grew, and we got new leadership. I then had the pleasure of working with one of the most amazing senior leaders I have ever met. Her name was Ronita Gaines. She was a Black woman (like me), very enthusiastic, and had a love of people unlike anyone I have ever seen. She also saw something in me, and before I knew it, she was coaching me, mentoring me, and encouraging me to become a leader. Soon after, a position opened up. This time I was courageous enough to apply and was slotted to lead a rather large team. Luckily for me, she was there every step of the way. Even if I needed her at 3:00 a.m. she would not hesitate to be there with me. She reminded me so much of my father, and it felt right. The principles integrity, humility, love, support, and tenacity that he had instilled in me were evident in the leadership skills Ronita reinforced for me. I knew I was in the right place. I quickly stepped out of my comfort zone, and my path changed from that point forward.

I first led a small team of about fifteen individuals and then moved on to lead a team of over 100 individuals, with six leaders reporting to me. While I was managing that group, I helped develop a new line of business. I was very successful as a people leader and had developed a team of leaders, but knew that there was more I still needed to do. It was time to embark on a different challenge.

I knew that no matter what that new challenge was, I still needed to be able to continue to develop leaders. Selfishly, this was more about me than them, and I'll explain why. Working with different individuals and helping develop them to be great leaders taught me more than I think I taught them. It challenged me, it forced me to be patient, it allowed me to cross-examine my leadership skills, and most importantly it instilled the idea of flexibility in approach. I have learned that leadership does not have a one-size-fits-all method; it takes time and understanding of people to be successful. And every person is different. This is often frustrating for new leaders, but the right guidance, direction and—if you are lucky—the right leadership will inspire you to do great things.

I then heard of a corporate training position open in account management, and I remember thinking that this is it; this is where I could focus on training and sharpening my skills. I had a great relationship with the hiring manager, who then immediately scheduled some time with me. I got the job and remain in love with it and the team I serve. I also work under a great woman leader who inspires me daily. Her support and genuine desire to serve her team as a vice president is inspiring. She truly puts people first and is focused on ensuring that we continue to develop great leaders under her. I am lucky to have found this path. These leaders continually serve as a sounding board for me and are a part of my mentors and sponsors tribe.

JULIET'S GREATEST CHALLENGE

When I first became a leader, I found it challenging to build rapport quickly. I was a very young, Black leader at the time, and I could actually see doubt in people's faces. Unfortunately, I initially had to prove I was worthy of being there. I was very aware of this, even prior to embarking on the journey, so I was ready to challenge myself to quickly connect with different individuals. I realized that I needed a plan, and I needed not only to hold myself accountable, but I also needed my team members to hold me accountable.

I needed a plan, so I wrote out an outline of my ninety-day plan. In the first thirty days, I was going to become an expert in the business, to learn as much as I could about the business as well as the team members. Days thirty-one through sixty were dedicated to having conversations with each team member about his or her goals and aspirations. This was really to understand them as individuals and why they chose to be there. The feedback I got from that fueled me further. Most people actually told me that they had have never had such a conversation with their leader and that they were appreciative of the time and effort. In days sixty-one through ninety, I was going to appoint leaders within the team. This did not mean that I had to open new positions, but I wanted everyone to at least lead a project that they enjoyed. There were a few team members who were comfortable where they were, and that was okay, too. My goal was to be able to take them eventually where they did not know they wanted to go. I understood this would take time. These activities over the first ninety days allowed me to earn the team's trust and gain momentum. From there on, I instituted open-door policies and surveys to ensure that the team felt empowered to keep me accountable. This methodology allowed people to start looking past my age as a leader, and I was then able to focus on performance.

When coaching leaders, I often get questions on how they can quickly build credibility. From my experience, especially if you are leading a new team or are new to the team, never skip earning their trust. Do not assume that your title automatically equals trust. A trusting team is a performing team. Your team needs to see you as a leader, and that means they must trust you to make decisions for them. This is critical. As Simon Sinek says, "Leadership is not about being in charge. Leadership is about taking care of those in your charge."

JULIET'S BEST ADVICE

I would say to any woman, "Trust yourself and remember that everyone is just trying to figure it out." Whenever imposter syndrome kicks in—and it will from time to time—remind yourself that you too will figure it out. Every leader today started somewhere when someone gave them a chance. Someone trusted them to lead, before they had any experience.

I will share a story about the first time I hired a leader I hired without experience. Going through the motions and posting positions, we typically have a conversation with HR about what the requirements should look like. And, generally, there are criteria, including years of experience. In my opinion, this actually deters people who want that shot. There are a few courageous souls (I was one of them) who apply anyway. One of them who came across my desk was a recent college grad who had some experience in the industry but did not have leadership experience. She had a note in her resume that called out that, regardless of lack of experience in leading teams, she had experience in leading projects, and there were some nuggets on why she thought she would be the best fit for the position. That intrigued me, as it reminded me of myself. I called her in for an interview. Her enthusiasm, charisma, and presence sold me. And once she was on the team, she grew to become a leader of leaders—and without having asked permission. This brings us back to the story of leading from where you are. How do you influence the people around you? How do you show up for the people around you?

Trust yourself, take that leap, take it one day at a time, and lead from where you are.

ABOUT JULIET

Juliet is a senior corporate trainer and loves helping people learn, grow, and lead. She has spent the majority of her career in the healthcare industry, gaining experiences in areas such as operations, process improvement, sales, and account management. While training is her primary job function by day, Juliet also enjoys growing in community with leaders and creating jewelry. She is the Vice President of the Phoenix chapter of Healthcare Business Women's Association, where she volunteers with other leaders in the industry to provide a platform for growth and development for women in healthcare and others. She also is the owner of KilohJewels, an online boutique where she sells her jewelry designs as well as other jewelers' designs. She also enjoys traveling and being with nature. Having lived on three continents, Juliet has a great love for people and an understanding of how to nurture and connect people using their strengths.

LISTEN TO THAT WISE INNER VOICE

Danielle Nava-Mijares
CEO, Nava Consulting LLC

DANIELLE'S PATH TO LEADERSHIP

My own path to leadership was an accidental one, if I'm honest. And my path continues to evolve as I evolve. I landed in my career at the age of twenty-two. I hired on as a specialist for a social justice nonprofit organization. It was a relatively flat organization with an executive director, board of directors, and everyone else as specialists. I had a lot of tenacity and perfectionism, and my saving grace was that I was a hard worker, curious, and brave. In those early years, I kept creating—programs, curricula, practices, and whatever else I thought I could offer. I wasn't trying to impress anyone.

I was in my zone of genius. I was in love with what I was doing. I was working mostly with students, at the time cocreating space with them to have dialogue about racism, discrimination, and bullying in a way that brought them together. I thought this was the best the work could ever get.

Over time, the organization created steppingstones for me: senior specialist, coordinator, and finally program director. I felt like I was making an unexpected mark in the world. I had no real experience of formal leadership. Everything I had done thus far was without any strategy to get ahead in the organization. I was too young in my career to even understand the possibilities of that happening. Becoming a director of our organization's largest and most financially secure program meant I'd be hiring, managing, working on pitches, closing with clients, presenting to funders and the Board, and going from peer to boss of my colleagues. No one and nothing prepared me for that experience. All I had under my belt to bring into this role was some successful and informal leadership experience. I believe there are personalities geared for natural leadership, but the rest of us have to really work at it. I am still working at it.

During this role change from peer to boss, I gained and lost respect and friends for various reasons (including not hiring a partner of a staff person), made enemies, and had narratives and accusations created about me White-centering and prioritizing White people's needs in a social justice organization. It was rough the first couple of years in that director's role. I went to graduate school and earned a master's in Organizational Leadership. After that, my approach to leadership was dramatically different.

Reflecting back reminds me of the powerful impact of informal leadership. Back then, I had no realization at the time that I was paving a new road of leadership opportunities in the organization. I helped to change the flat organization to one that was more of a hierarchy. I helped create opportunities for upward mobility, but I also ended up suppressing the creativity of the ebb and flow that once was present. The freedom of informal leadership was no longer wide open with this new organizational chart. Simply, there is unintended loss in things gained. I stayed with this organization for over a decade. I exited knowing I had created platforms and best practices that continued long after I left the organization. A few people I hired are still there twenty-plus years later in executive leadership positions. I like to think that inexperienced leadership efforts weren't a total wreck during those first years of my leader's journey.

Moving forward, every place I accepted employment after that first job was at the executive management level. Despite my failures, perceived and real, I had a reputation for having content expertise and being collaborative and knowledgeable about the work. I was recognized as a leader in my field. I was writing and publishing papers, and researching. I received a governor's appointment to the Fair Housing and Employment Commission and wrote policy that benefited women. I was presenting at the national level on diversity and equity issues, and serving and leading on boards of directors at the state and local levels. I landed an adjunct faculty position that allowed me academic freedom to explore the topics of oppression, antibias, antiracism, and the educational gap. This added to my credibility in the workplace, community, and larger social justice arenas. The opportunities kept coming, and I kept saying yes. I was doing the work, and yet I still didn't know much about leading outside of my studies, except by example. I learned being a good worker didn't necessarily translate to being a good leader.

In all of this, I found a beautiful mentor, Tina. She was a transformational leader before that term was spoken aloud. I was a servant leader, and my philosophy clashed with the transactional leadership styles that seemed to be in abundance. I learned a lot of leadership examples from Tina. Some of her strategies I was able to make my own, but Tina had a gentleness about her that must be authentic and not fabricated. I couldn't master her gentleness without stifling myself. Some people gravitated to her gentle yet powerful style, and others thought she was too soft. I learned a lasting lesson from her. Even the best leaders can't be all things to all people.

I went on to work for three more organizations, this time at the national level, before landing in what would be the last nonprofit I would serve as full-time staff before branching out on my own. The last organization nearly broke me. I experienced spirit-crushing examples of poor leadership. I was often asked to compromise my values. I was often torn down, made to feel invisible, disrespected, and not included in leadership decisions until after they were executed. I was a part of executive leadership in name only. Yet, my contributions were financially and programmatically significant to the organization. I attribute being able to produce because of my personal leadership philosophy as a servant leader. However, this experience led me to make the most powerful and terrifying professional decision I ever made. After seven years, I resigned. I simply gave two weeks and left with both joy and fear.

This past year, I celebrated my twenty-fifth anniversary in social justice/education work. This coming May, I will celebrate four years of the birth of my consulting firm. In the past three-and-a-half years, I've built a real business. I turned myself from consultant into a CEO of both my life and business. My work is 90% referral based. What's this have to do with leadership? It's a reminder that leadership isn't always top down and there are many ways to lead.

I know I am better as a person and a leader when I am working in collaboration as a partner, rather than leading a staff of people. When I invite people to work with me on projects, that's exactly what it is. It's an invitation to step into or stay in their zone of genius under their own name; marrying our concepts, skills, and strengths; and creating amazing outcomes and serving our clients at the highest level.

My leadership roles now are in more collaborative styles and spaces. I am a more creative leader now and am more committed to being authentic about what type of work I want to do. As a truth seeker, I did the work to discover my deeper truth about wanting to be of service and about committing my life work to antibias and antiracist education. I know my deepest truths, the whys for my work, and how I want to show up in my leadership. This makes it much easier to pick partners to work with, and it's easier to know when to say "no thank you." Authentic, collaborative, and service-based leadership brings out the best in me and my work. Being able to stand in my truth about how I want to work with others has been the best discovery in my leadership journey.

DANIELLE'S GREATEST CHALLENGE

The only images I had of professionals in leadership roles were of white men. Brilliant women playing small to accommodate the gendered realities that many capable women face were often the examples I took my lead from. My greatest challenge as a leader was feeling like I had to lead like a man. My brain wasn't wired to do that. Racially and ethnically, my spirit wasn't in alignment either to lead in this way I was being groomed. As a woman of color, my professional experiences were shaped by white male leaders, and I was advised by them on how to act, speak, approach, and be. When I encountered female leaders, they were white, and they too had advice on how to be more like them. In my formative professional years, success—even working in the social justice arena—meant that I had to look, speak, and behave in ways that were acceptable to those in leadership.

To some degree, my voice and intuition were silenced on occasion. I didn't know I was assimilating. I found myself compromising and losing a part of my design, creativity, and intuition the higher I moved into leadership roles. I spent a lot of time trying to diagnose why I felt out of alignment; why I felt like I was having "the emperor has no clothes" moments in staff meetings. I would look around the table and see heads nodding in agreement as though we were experts on approaches to working with communities of color where we would be uninvited guests. I decided to address this challenge and other problems.

First, I had to decide that my own safety in the organization was less important than the well-being and needs of the people we were serving. I approached my direct supervisor, the one who had been my peer before I was hired in the organization. He was the same person who brought me to the executive director to advocate my being hired. I asked him for time to talk. I told him I needed a courageous conversation with him. The conversation had its highs and lows. It was filled with laughter too, some respect, admiration, and understanding of each other. I thanked him for his time, and he said he appreciated the opportunity to hear how there may be different solutions and approaches to consider. The next morning, I learned that he reported me to our executive director for insubordination. That insubordination report turned into a productive conversation about approaches to our community work. We made changes, recruiting and paying community members to participate in our brainstorming and development sessions. We created a process that was inclusive and that met the needs the community identified themselves. We changed our approach with humility and gratitude for those who helped us get it better.

What I am reminded of is the archaic double standard that speaking your truth, as a woman, can get you in trouble, but it can also reap amazing outcomes. I trust myself to speak up. I do it with compassion and from a place of good, not ego. I do it with the idea that relationships are paramount and are best built when truths are shared for better outcomes and stronger connections.

DANIELLE'S BEST ADVICE

I am going to say something contradictory here, but hear me out.

Invest in a coach, whether it be financially, in terms of time, or both. A coach invites you to do work; the coach doesn't do it for you. A great coach will help you to discover the barriers and blocks to your own success. A coach isn't a therapist, but after a session, you may feel like your load feels lighter or that the answers you were looking for become very apparent. Now the contradiction: Take time to pause and reflect on what's happening for you in the work and in your life's work (sometimes they are the same). Get uncomfortable with your own rumble and anxiety. Stop looking for outside perspectives, validation, reinforcements, or justifications.

Dig into that inner wisdom that lives in our bodies—advice from our ancestors, teachings from experience, and some curated by friendly advice. Trust your voice. Be your own mentor. Keep your eyes and ears wide open to what your gut and heart say; they do not lie. Listen to that wise inner voice that lives in you.

The only other piece of advice I offer is to say a resounding YES to the opportunities that you didn't anticipate. Our lives—all of our different parts that make up our lives—are interdependent. One *yes* can change the trajectory of all the parts of your life. Unless you're being chased by a bobcat, walk past the fear of the unknown. Say yes to things that have opportunity to make your heart sing and voice shake a little. This way you allow your genius the possibilities to reveal itself, over and over and over again.

ABOUT DANIELLE

Danielle Nava-Mijares is an antibias and antiracist educator and educational strategist. Danielle started her consulting firm, Nava Consulting LLC, in 2017, after a twenty-five-year career in the nonprofit sector. Previously, she served in program and executive management leadership at local, state, and national nonprofit organizations focused on social justice issues.

Danielle's work is specialized in the area of diversity, and inclusion, and higher education. She designs and facilitates professional development trainings for organizations, schools, and universities, and provides coaching for executive leadership to do the uncomfortable work of dismantling oppressive systems. She also coaches teachers looking to become antiracist educators.

Danielle brings expertise in human relations, restorative mediation, organizational leadership, and nonverbal communication. She is a certified both as a Conflict Mediator and a Body Language Specialist. She has over 150 hours of restorative justice training and practice. She has been adjunct faculty at Chapman University (2002–2013) and California State University, Fullerton (2019–).

Danielle also has a coaching practice within her firm. She is an accountability coach for women who need support with strategic alignment of professional and personal goals.

Danielle has been recognized at local levels by city councils, Los Angeles County, and local organizations for her contributions to community and education. In 2007, she was named an American Marshall Memorial Fellow and traveled across the Atlantic to help strengthen our relations with various European countries. In 2009, Cypress College recognized her as Alumna of the Year. In 2012, Danielle received a Governor's appointment and served on the Fair Employment and Housing Commission, where she coauthored new pregnancy regulations.

Danielle lives in Orange County with her husband and their son. She is an avid community volunteer. Currently she is appointed by her city council members to serve on her city's Citizen's Community Development Committee. She is cochair of this committee, which is responsible for reviewing and recommending nonprofit funding proposals for Community Development Block Grant funds. She is a book lover and iced tea drinker, and swears by the perfect paper planner and pens.

LEADERSHIP IS NOT ALWAYS AN ENTREPRENEUR OR A CEO

Jamie Weaver
Director of Business Development

JAMIE'S PATH TO LEADERSHIP

"How did you end up in your current position?" This is my favorite networking question. You can learn a lot about a person from the answer. A majority of the people have a very diverse career path that somehow comes together to make them perfectly qualified for their current role. My career path story is similar to theirs.

When I was growing up, my adult role models were my father, my grandfathers, and my uncles. They all worked in different industries, but they all had skills that were needed. They were all good at what they did, and they put in a hard day of work for their wages. There were no games. In their line of work, a task was either done or it was not done. This began my fascination with the trades.

My father worked in the blast furnace at the local steel mill and owned a portable welding service. I followed in his footsteps and earned my associate's degree in welding technologies. My first real job was as a pipe fitter, root welding rolled and welded culvert pipe.

My mother had worked in a department store, and during my high school years, I worked with her. I was comfortable talking with people and finding what they needed.

I decided to try and blend the two worlds and went into steel sales. It was a comfortable transition for me because I knew the product and I enjoyed helping clients. Then I got married and had children. My husband earned a good living, and my hours and commute were too much for our family; so I gave up my job.

There was an opportunity in the paper to work part-time from home in the rendering industry. This was an old, established company that was the chief local provider of rendering. They had never had a salesperson, but things were changing. There were now more competitors, and the competition was advertising and introducing contractual agreements. I was fortunate enough to start at the ground level, finding resources and putting together systems to target new food-service locations opening in our target region.

Then I took a job in commercial pest control, working with health-care, education, restaurant, hospitality, office, and multifamily properties. I earned my certification in entomology from Purdue University, surpassed my goals every month, and pushed past my comfort zone by addressing hospital boards, immersing myself in associations, and providing staff training. It could have been a dream job, but the company culture was not a fit for me. I did complete one year there and resigned on my anniversary date. Because my free time is filled with kids and horses, when I left this position, I used my last paycheck to buy a horse trailer.

My current role is where these diverse paths came together. A friend from the horse barn invited my family to her Christmas party. She introduced me to the owner of an eighty-five-year-old commercial roofing company, specializing in new-construction roofs and reroofing existing buildings for all industries. The company put on amazing roofs, but they needed to get their name out into the community, which was the same region I had always worked in! They needed to create a whole new system and list of clients. This position was the perfect fit for me. All of the different experiences I had had, the people I had met, the industries I had worked in came together to bring value.

Leadership is not always manifested in an entrepreneur or CEO. Many times, it emerges in volunteers or other people willing to provide whatever value they can offer to make an industry better.

JAMIE'S GREATEST CHALLENGE

My greatest challenge has been discovering what value I can offer. I have read that you need to bring value to your employer and your clients. I am not a professional roofer; I have nothing to give them, I think. Then I remind myself that *being myself* is my value. I specialize in business development and marketing. My skills are developing new business and marketing the company. I am not an imposter because I know my job well; my perspective and priorities are unique. You can be expected to be good at your specific role, and *actually being good at it* is something you can be proud of. This is true for all positions. My father, grandfather, and uncles would agree.

Nurture your knowledge. My roofing knowledge, though seriously lacking compared with a professional roofer's, is more than most people's. I do study roofing products and techniques, and attend industry events. But I know and respect my limitations. I ask the professional roofers to review any technical information before it is released.

Adding value can be as simple as offering coworkers my respect and turning in receipts promptly to accounting. There are count-less ways to add value that do not cost a dime. Remember to treat people like people: interact with customers' social media posts, answer that email, attend their events, make conversation, be a bright spot in their day.

JAMIE'S BEST ADVICE

I have not met many leaders who were tapped on the shoulder and told they could be a leader. I have met many leaders who saw a need and jumped in and addressed it. They are usually the first to volunteer. Leadership is not glamorous; it is not a title or a giant paycheck. Leaders are on the front line, making things easier for the rest of the team. They do not always have the executive title of a leader. They are the ones that listen and care. They notice what is happening in the workplace. What are the pain points? Where is there a disconnect? How can those gaps be bridged? What tools can you use to fix it? Everyone has problems and ideas about how to fix it. A leader has a solution, a strategy, and implements it. The plan may not always work, or it may be a slow process, but risk and failure are a part of success. Keep your team's best interest at heart. Success is helping others achieve their goals. Nobody cares until they know how much you care. I guarantee that nobody cares that you want to be a leader. You will need to learn to believe in yourself and that what you are doing is helping someone.

An old friend gave me this advice: when you enter a meeting, picture your whole company walking in with you. This tip will give you the confidence to represent them well.

ABOUT JAMIE

Jamie Weaver is the Director of Business Development for Geissler Roofing Co., Inc., specializing in securing commercial roofing and siding projects for the company. She got her Associate of Applied Science in Welding Technologies from a community college and went to work as a pipe fitter. Her talents and ability to learn new skills propelled her into a twenty-plus-year career of helping blue-collar craftsman who are very good at their craft be more visible and secure the business they deserved. She saw a gap between the master craftsman and the well-marketed businesses and wanted to help the better business win. Since accepting her current role in commercial roofing, she has become chair for the Specialty Contractors Council for the Associated General Contractors (AGC) of Missouri. Her firm was awarded the AGC1st award and is currently being considered for a Keystone project award. She is always learning new skills to keep up with the industry and recently earned several certificates from Disney University.

Jamie strongly believes that marketing and business development work hand–in hand. Neither function should be complicated or expensive. The world has changed, and people are looking for honesty and transparency. The internet and social media have allowed small businesses to compete with the corporate Goliaths…and win.

RECOGNIZE YOUR PATH AND RISE UP

Deneen L. Garrett
Talent Development + Diversity Lead and Podcast Creator/Host

DENEEN'S PATH TO LEADERSHIP

As I prepared for my move from Detroit, Michigan to Las Vegas, Nevada, in 2008, I prayed to learn my purpose and passion. After being there for a few months, I was invited to participate in the Employee Resource Group (ERG) conference that was hosted by the telecommunications company for which I worked, and after attending, I knew I wanted a career in Diversity and Inclusion (D&I). Over the next five years, I led several ERG initiatives, increased the membership of both our ERGs and volunteer organization, and hosted mentoring circles, in addition to leading a team of fifteen customer advocates, who consistently ranked in the top three under my leadership. Additionally, I built relationships with individuals on the D&I team and made key decision makers aware of my desire to have a career in D&I. A few months after telling my then Chief Diversity Officer I wanted a role in D&I, I interviewed for and was offered the role. I've held it now for almost five years.

My then role as a D&I professional allowed me to passionately pursue my purpose daily. It provided me the platform to create opportunities for others, develop programs, lead events, and create and moderate panels. While thinking about how to level-up, I launched the An Intimate Conversation with Women of Color podcast to provide Women of Color a platform to use their voices. This grew out of the panel I created and moderated for three years at an external event. From panel to podcast, this is my journey which has me on over seven platforms including Spotify, iHeart Radio, and Amazon Music. When I recorded my first episode, I committed to producing one episode per month, which immediately turned into one episode per week. I actually have guests lined up five months out.

It thrills me to see my reach expand beyond the United States to such far-flung places as Malaysia, Slovakia, and Germany, where a colleague, who has become one of my biggest advocates, listens to the podcast on her runs. At the time of this writing, I'm listened to on multiple platforms and in more than twenty countries with Nigeria being the country that is home to one of the newest additions to my listenership as of the time of this writing. I am truly international as, as of January 2021, I have had a guest from the United Kingdom and have a guest from France scheduled to make an appearance on my podcast.

I have a dedicated Facebook group, website, and LinkedIn page named An Intimate Conversation with Women of Color, and I am active across several social media platforms to include Instagram and Twitter as @IntimatewithWOC. My vision of empowering millions of women is moving at full speed.

DENEEN'S GREATEST CHALLENGE

My greatest challenge as a leader is working with people who underestimate and/or are intimidated by me. I was recently described as a "fierce ally," which describes how I approach my work: I am fierce; I am passionate; I am confident. Some might be intimidated by my being a woman—especially, a Black woman. That's not my issue. I refuse to dim my light for others. I live to make a difference in the lives of others so that my light brightens their path. My coach told me that if he and I said the same thing to the same people, some would only receive it from me; therefore, I will continue to use my voice in the manner I do.

Not everyone who is in a leadership position has leadership capabilities. Sometimes these people try to box you in. They're frustrated by their own lack of movement, so they do little to help you along. As a self-starter, I've just had to move around these people and create my own opportunities. Having mentors also comes in handy.

Now, more and more people ask me to use my voice. They want to hear what I have to say. In 2020, I was positioned to be the voice of an organization. I was recommended based on how I use my voice inside and outside of work.

Being true to myself, remaining authentic, using my voice, championing for others, and creating my own opportunities are how I overcome challenges or pathways to growth. I continue to use my gifts for the good of others and myself, and the blessings I'm to receive will come in their own time. I believe feedback is a gift. You choose what to do with gifts, and I choose to take the parts that will strengthen me.

DENEEN'S BEST ADVICE

The first thing I tell the many people whom I coach and mentor is to decide what it is they want. This is the starting point. Once you know this, you can chart your path. This is an exploratory exercise, and many don't have an answer. That's fine. Just know you must get to work figuring it out. Ask yourself these questions:

- What brings me joy?

- What do I do without thinking about it?

- When I lose time doing something, what is it I'm doing?

- What comes naturally to me?

- What gifts do others seen in me?

Write down your answers, keep a journal, reflect, and pray. Once you have clarity, create an action plan. Connect with people who are doing what you want to do. Pick their brains. Read their LinkedIn profiles and biographies. Volunteer to get experience. Let key decision-makers know what you're interested in doing. Share what you've done to reach your goal(s). Ask if you can stay connected, provide them with updates, and ask them to advocate for you.

Relationships are key to life. They are about who you know and most importantly who knows you. Become a thought leader, write a blog, publish article, be a guest on podcasts—or start your own. Image and exposure are paramount. Get a personal board of directors, which at the time of this writing is a goal of mine. Surround yourself with people who will help guide you, correct you, and celebrate YOU!

Also recognize your path is just that—YOURS. Learn from others, and let them motivate you; but do not compare yourself to them. There are women who launched their podcasts after I launched mine and have many plays/downloads. I could let this bother me, or I can recognize that I'm on a journey and that my journey will be an example to others. My experiences are part of my story. Not only did I pray to know my purpose and passion, I also prayed that my moving to Las Vegas would encourage others to take a leap. If I get what I want without making any effort, I will have nothing to tell others, nothing motivational or encouraging to share.

Since launching my podcast, I've had many "catch up to the vision" moments. These are revelations of what's to come. Just before Christmas 2020, I was given a program to manage, a program in which I had been wanting to participate. Instead of just being a participant, I'm leading it!

To rise is to ascend, or more directly, it is to start from somewhere. Enjoy your journey and rise up! I once shared a post on LinkedIn of several women with the words "inspire," "resist," and "discover," encouraging others to think about which one they wanted to embody for the rest of 2020 and into 2021. I chose "soar." To soar is to move upward "toward a higher place, point, or level." Onward and upward!!!

ABOUT DENEEN

Deneen L. Garrett is a known as a natural motivator and coach with a passion for Diversity, Equity and Inclusion (D&I) and a gift for innovation and execution (her piece of the **PIE**). This talent cultivator excels at improving professional development for marginalized employees and whose contributions and relationships led  to her company being named one of their partner's 2019 Corporations of the Year.

Deneen rapidly rose through her early career as she earned promotions from Customer Service Advocate to Sales Support Manager to Lead Sales Support Manager and to Sales Order Quality Project Manager roles from 2000 to 2006 at a global telecommunications company. Promoted yet again in 2009 to Customer Service Manager-Internet Services, her process improvement and operational strengths quickly became evident via her leadership of a team of twenty serving a customer base of 17,000. She built out a digital pilot program that drove customer experience from fourth to first quintiles and achieved +90% call efficiency, +81% necessary dispatch, and 67% improvement in thirty days. By redirecting the call center's focus and leveraging customer service and product training, she catalyzed a 200% revenue gain.

Named Manager of Entertainment Group in 2013, she realized similar productivity growth for a 100-person vendor management group while outpacing performance metrics by 100% and carving out $2 million in annual savings. Deneen also developed and facilitated a leadership development program for non-managers and championed mentoring with a group of 200-member management staff.

Elevated to Lead Diversity Consultant in 2016 to leverage talent acquisition, employee development, and sponsorship initiatives on behalf of the company's diverse employees, she co-founded the company's first-ever Inclusion Council and led D&I projects impacting employees globally.

As of January 2021, Deneen leads the WOC Program for her company and has the responsibility of building out this program which now encompasses several programs in one.

Through her leadership of diversity, equity, and inclusion programs spanning multiple employee segments, Deneen L. Garrett serves as a key culture change advocate and best practices champion. She rolled out a staff development and mentorship program that generated participant promotions, hosted career programs for college students, and led executive leadership tours with Hispanic and Latino staff. Her efforts expanded sponsorships and more than doubled attendance of a panel she created over a three-year period.

Deneen activated an LGBTQ+ suicide prevention initiative and boosted diversity hires 90% by employing a range of non-traditional recruiting practices.

Most recently Deneen launched the An Intimate Conversation with Women of Color podcast. Through her podcast, Deneen seeks to empower and to elevate the voices of Women of Color.

Deneen earned her Master of Science Administration General Administration degree from Central Michigan University and her Bachelor of Science in Criminal Justice from Wayne State University. She has earned Six Sigma White and Yellow Belts and is certified in Quality Management System Lean. Her writing has been showcased as part of the DBP Members Celebrate Hispanic Heritage Month, the AISES Winds of Change Professional Development series and internally for various segment communications. Her honors include Top 3 in Sales, President's Club for Sales, and the U.S. President's Volunteer Service Award (10+ times). Deneen, along with her colleagues, participated in a contest in which they won and received company-wide recognition for the solution they created.

LEADERSHIP IS MORE THAN A JOB TITLE

Noelymari Sanchez Velez

Business Operations Administrator and Public Relations Director

A leader is one who takes the initiative, who sees beyond the task at hand, who is empathetic, who motivates, and who connects with others. When it came to my work, I felt it was not the same until opportunities were presented and I was working alongside leaders who showed me the way. Ever since I can remember, I have taken the initiative to lead in my life. I am thankful for my family as they have been my #1 fans, cheering me on to always accomplish anything I set my mind to.

NOELYMARI'S PATH TO LEADERSHIP

In 1999, I began my journey in the nonprofit world with Community Partners in Action (CPA) in Hartford, Connecticut. Formerly called the Connecticut Prison Association, CPA has been around since 1875 with the core belief that people can change and that all humans—even if they've been incarcerated—deserve dignity and the right to be treated fairly.

For three years I worked as the Administrative Assistant at two of our programs, providing assistance to the population we serve. At CPA, we are advocates for rethinking and improving the criminal justice system, and our programs truly provide people with the tools and skills they need to succeed. CPA champions criminal justice reform and advocates for preserving human dignity. Through our programs, which include reentry and housing, youth initiatives, a nationally recognized Prison Arts Program, and holistic alternatives to incarceration, we provide long-term impact that positively transforms individuals and society at large.

In 2002, I applied for and was promoted to the position of Executive Assistant to the Executive Director of the agency. I was in this role for more than sixteen years, and during this time, I was provided with different responsibilities to take the lead in coordinating events, working on different agency projects, working closely with our Board of Directors, and maintaining the efficiency of the day-to-day office operations.

In a conversation I had with our HR Director a few years ago, we discussed my role. She referenced how I had been taking on a leadership role, however, I did not think of myself as a leader, as I did not have a leadership job title. She mentioned how I had been taking the initiative in projects and leading our team on numerous occasions. My work, my passion, and how I led were being noticed.

Before this conversation, I had not seen my role as one of leadership. This conversation helped me set forth new professional goals as I was asked to take on additional responsibilities within the agency. I decided to go back to school to study Organizational Leadership, which allowed me to obtain a better understanding of the responsibilities and tasks for which I was responsible. In addition, I was asked to take a course on project management and became the agency's Lead Project Manager.

Most recently, in 2019, I was promoted to Business Operations Administrator and now have additional responsibilities of managing and leading major projects agency-wide (e.g., IT projects such as Office 365 migration and the implementation of Microsoft Teams and Salesforce, a data management software). In my role, I work closely with the agency's Executive Director, HR, Fiscal, Development, and IT as part of the Executive Leadership Team, and I assist with their projects when needed.

In addition to my position with CPA, I work alongside my husband as the Public Relations Director for our photography business, JCV Freelance Photography, LLC. It is one of my greatest joys to collaborate and work with my husband. We are very proud of being at the helm of a minority-owned business. Bringing innovative and creative ways to stay current and to provide the best service we can to our customers are of utmost important to us.

NOELYMARI'S GREATEST CHALLENGE

One of my greatest challenges as a leader was acquiring new skill sets that were outside of my comfort zone. I addressed this by immersing myself in learning about these new skills, becoming more efficient and diverse.

One of my personality traits is to think through a problem or issue and make a decision that will be beneficial to all, not just me. This has helped me in my roles to be able to consider all who are involved in working with me and how making the right decisions will benefit all.

Working alongside others and having certain expectations may not be easy at times. When working independently, you take responsibility and control of your own actions and decisions. As a leader, you must also effectively interact, cooperate, collaborate, manage conflicts, and learn about the working styles of your team. You must do it with grace while making everyone around you feel comfortable.

In the world of COVID-19, we all had to adjust and continue to lead our teams with grace and encouragement. Working remotely has its challenges, but making sure your team is provided with the tools to perform at their best is essential.

NOELYMARI'S BEST ADVICE

Take the shot! To lead does not mean that you have to be in a leadership position; it means that you have the confidence to take the initiative to learn all you can about the work that you do and where you see yourself leading. As you prepare for your career, have an understanding of the path you want to take, learning as much as you can and attaining different skill sets. This will allow you to understand others on your team and how you can best help them.

Never think you are superior to others. Being a leader is not about what you say but how your actions demonstrate your true leadership and ability to offer guidance to others. I take pride in the goals I have set and accomplished. The work of a leader is not about independence but about collaboration with others. Do not shy away from trying or from learning and going the extra mile; it will get noticed.

I've had the blessing of having mentors in my life who have guided me and encouraged me to always seek beyond the obvious. Ask for or find a mentor who can guide you and be an inspiration to you, but do not forget to do the same for other women along the way in your career, always paying it forward.

ABOUT NOELYMARI

Noelymari Sanchez Velez has more than twenty years of experience at a 145-year-old nonprofit criminal justice agency based in Hartford, Connecticut. Noelymari gained experience as an Administrative Assistant for two of the agency's programs. She worked as the Executive Assistant and Project Manager and currently serves as the agency's Business Operations Administrator.

She attended Manchester Community College and The American Women's College at Bay Path University. She holds a Certification in Project Management from Post University.

Since 2017, Noelymari Sanchez Velez has worked with her husband, Julio, as owners of JCV Freelance Photography, LLC, based in East Hartford, Connecticut. She is the Public Relations Director and the Wedding Officiant. She oversees customer service, contracts, and day-of coordination. She and her husband engage in a healthy lifestyle by staying active along with sharing a mutual love for photography.

In 2020, Noelymari became a Published Author through the *Transformation 2020* book anthology that provides twenty inspiring stories of power and healing from women leaders. In August 2020, she was awarded the 100 Women of Color Award for her work in the community. She and her husband have volunteered their time with Connecticut's Department of Children and Families as photographers for the National Adoption Day since 2017 and for DCF's Heart Gallery of America, capturing the individuality and dignity of children living in foster care in an effort to raise public awareness about their needs.

Noelymari is a native of Puerto Rico and has lived in Connecticut for almost thirty years.

ABOUT THE EDITORS

BRIDGETT MCGOWEN-HAWKINS

"Talks too much" was a comment Bridgett consistently received on her elementary school report cards, and seldom did she ever go anywhere as a child without a book or a dictionary in her hand. Early on, she developed a love for speaking and the written word—so much so that she was always the first to volunteer to read passages aloud in class, and during moments of boredom in her third- and fourth-grade classes, she would analyze the dictionary, jotting down those words and definitions she found particularly interesting.

With reading as a favorite pastime and little to no fear of speaking in front of a crowd, it only makes sense that Bridgett is now an award-winning international professional speaker; an award-winning author; and the CEO of BMcTALKS Press, an independent publishing company, where she thrives in an environment that positions her to bring other people's words to life. Bridgett's résumé also includes being a 2019–2020 member of Forbes Coaches Council and launching BMcTALKS Academy, where, as the founder and owner, she offers online, self-paced courses to move professionals to use their voices to monetize their expertise.

Since 2001, Bridgett has been a professional speaker, and she has appeared on programs alongside several prominent figures such as former President Barack Obama, Deepak Chopra, Alex Rodriguez (A-Rod), Oprah Winfrey, Shonda Rhimes, Katie Couric, Chip Gaines, Janelle Monáe, and Amy Cuddy.

The prestigious University of Texas at Austin presented her with a Master Presenter Award in 2006; Canada-based One Woman has presented her with two Fearless Woman Awards; and she has facilitated hundreds of workshops, keynote and commencement addresses, conference sessions, trainings, and webinars to thousands of students and professionals who are positioned all around the globe.

Bridgett's expertise and presentations have been sought after by companies, post-secondary institutions, and organizations such as Society for Human Resource Management (SHRM), Vanguard Investments, Norton LifeLock, Symantec, Kentucky Fried Chicken,

McGraw-Hill Education, LinkedIn Local, Association for Talent Development (ATD), Doña Ana Community College, North Carolina Chamber of Commerce, National Association of Women Sales Professionals, Independence University, Arizona Private School Association, Turnitin, Texas Healthcare Trustees, National Association of Black Accountants, Greater Phoenix Convention & Visitors Bureau, and Prairie View A&M University.

Forbes, Entrepreneur, LinkedIn, and *Thrive Global* are a few of the platforms where you can find articles penned by Bridgett. In addition, she has been quoted by Transizion, has contributed to UpJourney, and has appeared as a guest on The Training and Learning Development Company's TLDCast, Phoenix Business Radio, and a multitude of podcasts to showcase her expertise in the professional speaking industry. Her work has been highlighted by *VoyagePhoenix Magazine*; award-winning Scottsdale-based branding and consulting agency Catalyst; The Startup Growth; and her alma mater, Prairie View A&M University (PVAMU), the second-oldest institution of higher education in the state of Texas and a part of the Texas A&M University System.

Bridgett has also taught for PVAMU, Lone Star College System, and University of Phoenix. She graduated cum laude with her bachelor's degree in communication, and one year later, she graduated summa cum laude with her master's degree.

Bridgett is a member of Entrepreneur Leadership Network; a member of International Society of Female Professionals; a member of Association for Talent Development; a former member of National Speakers Association; and a member of Alpha Kappa Alpha Sorority, Incorporated.

In 2019, Bridgett authored and published two books, *REAL TALK: What Other Experts Won't Tell You About How to Make Presentations That Sizzle* as well as *Rise and Sizzle: Daily Communication and Presentation Strategies for Sales, Business, and Higher Ed Pros*, the former of which was a finalist for a 2020 Next Generation Indie Book Award and won the 2020 Best Indie Book Award in the Non-Fiction: Business Leadership and Communications category.

In January 2020, she also wrote and published *Show Up and Show Out: 52 Communication Habits to Make You Unforgettable*, which sold out at the annual Think Better Live Better event hosted in February 2020 in San Diego, California, by *New York Times* best-sellers Marc and Angel Chernoff. Days later, she published her first compilation, *Own the Microphone: How 50 of the World's Best Professional Speakers Launched Their Careers (and How You Can, Too!)* Four months later, in June 2020, her second, third, and fourth compilations, *Triumph Over the Trials, Redesign Your 9-to-5*, and *A Collective Breath*, were published. Her first podcast, Own the Microphone, made its official debut in August 2020.

Bridgett's mission is to work beyond the hours of 9 a.m. to 5 p.m. to help scores of professionals turn their words and voices into powerhouses, inspire millions, and build serious skill sets and mindsets that will lead to more and more opportunities.

Bridgett is married to Aaron Hawkins, and he makes her laugh every day. Their family resides in the Phoenix, Arizona, area. Bridgett enjoys frequent summertime getaways to San Diego, and she absolutely loves beautiful sunsets.

SIMONE E. MORRIS

Simone E. Morris is CEO of Simone Morris Enterprises LLC, a certified minority- and women-owned business enterprise providing leadership solutions. She is an award-winning diversity and inclusion leader, recognized by Diversity Best Practices, Diversity MBA, *Diversity MBE Magazine*, and her former employer.
The Stevie® Awards for Women in Business recently dubbed her the 2020 Bronze Winner for Female Solo Entrepreneur of the Year.

Ms. Morris spent twenty-three years in corporate America in retail and the consumer products, financial, pharmaceutical, and information technology industries. Her work in the Diversity and Inclusion field began through leadership in an employee resource group, followed by a Human Resources role. Today Ms. Morris is a consultant, trainer, coach, and speaker committed to developing more inclusive leaders and creating authentic, inclusive cultures in organizations.

She holds an MBA from the University of Connecticut and is a certified Coach and Project Management Professional. Ms. Morris has received the Certificate of Mastery in the DEI program Cultivating Cultures of Inclusion & High Performance. Additionally, she has completed the Diversity and Inclusion Education and Training Course at Cornell. She is an Adjunct Assistant Professor of Public Service for NYU│Wagner. Her company, Simone Morris

Enterprises, is an authorized vendor for the Human Resource Certification Institute and Society for Human Resource Management.

Ms. Morris has written for *Entrepreneur, Forbes, The Good Men Project, Medium, American Management Association Playbook, Thrive Global, Profiles in Diversity Journal, Glassdoor, Leadercast, SmartRecruiters, Social Hire, Living Out Loud,* and *Diversity Best Practices.* She is also the author of *52 Tips for Owning Your Career: Practical Advice for Career Success, The Power of Owning Your Career: Winning Strategies, Tools, and Tips for Creating Your Desired Career,* and *Achievement Unlocked: Strategies to Set Goals and Manifest Them.* She is a featured contributor for *A Collective Breath, Own the Microphone,* and *Redesign Your 9-to-5* and is the co-editor and co-compiler of *Upward.*

She resides in Connecticut with her family.

ABOUT BMCTALKS PRESS

BMcTALKS Press is an independent publishing company that provides a full suite of publishing services to new authors with an emphasis on academicians, professional speakers, professional coaches, entrepreneurs, consultants, and small business owners.

We design, create, and deliver high-quality trade books and eBooks that expand your brand, support your vision, and solidify you as a contender in your industry.

BMcTALKS Press knows you are passionate about what you do. We empower you to realize the expertise, savviness, acumen, and passion you bring to the world, and we assist you with identifying avenues for achieving the goal of becoming a published author.

When you get published, you position yourself to …

- Add "published author" to your already impressive list of accomplishments
- Establish yourself as an authority on a topic
- Have a book that serves as an "elevated business card"
- Provide added value to your clients
- Support and expand your brand
- Give your followers another way to connect with you
- Share an important message with the world
- Position yourself to book (more) speaking engagements
- Leave a legacy
- Grow your business
- Be seen as an expert in your industry
- Make an impact

Visit **www.bmtpress.com** to schedule your no-obligation call to discuss your book idea.

Do you already have a completed manuscript?
Submit it to **info@bmtpress.com**, and let us get to work for you.

Made in the USA
Coppell, TX
11 March 2021